COLLABORATIONS:
ENGLISH IN OUR LIVES

Intermediate 2 Student Book

The publication of *Collaborations* was directed by the members of the Heinle & Heinle Secondary and Adult ESL Publishing Team:

Editorial Director: Roseanne Mendoza
Senior Production Services Coordinator: Lisa McLaughlin
Market Development Director: Andy Martin

Also participating in the publication of the program were:

Vice President and Publisher ESL: Stanley Galek
Senior Assistant Editor: Sally Conover
Production Editor: Maryellen Killeen
Manufacturing Coordinator: Mary Beth Hennebury
Full Service Design and Production: PC&F, Inc.
Illustration Program: G. Brian Karas and PC&F, Inc.

Manufactured in the United States of America.

ISBN: 0-8384-6634-6

Heinle & Heinle is a division of International Thomson Publishing, Inc.

Photo Credits

Cover: David Moss, top; Jean Bernard, center left; Corpus Christi Literacy Council, center middle; Thai-Hung Pham Nguyen, center right; © Jonathan Stark/Heinle & Heinle Publishers, bottom.

Unit 1: Jean Bernard, 1, 4 bottom, 5, 6, 8, 9 left and top right, 13 bottom left; Mike Johnson, 2, 4 top; Mariano Ramos Hernandez (book cover), 7; Peter Lee, 9 middle right; © Jonathan Stark/Heinle & Heinle Publishers, 9; Ulli Stetzler, 13; David Moss, 15.

Unit 2: Jeanne H. Schmedlen, 19, 20, 21, 23, 24; Thai-Hung Pham Nguyen, 25; Corpus Christi Literacy Council, 26, 32.

Unit 3: David Moss, 35, 36, 38, 40, 42, 45 top, 47 bottom; Jean Bernard, 45 bottom; Marie H. Bias, 47 top.

Unit 4: Greater Corpus Christi Business Alliance, 51; Corpus Christi Literacy Council, 52; AP/Wide World Photos, 53; Betty Lynch, 56, 57, 58; © King Photography/FPG, 62 top; © C. Peter Borsari/FPG, 62 bottom; © Kozlowski Productions/FPG, 63; © Jonathan Stark/Heinle & Heinle Publishers, 65.

Unit 5: David Moss, 69 right and bottom, 70, 71, 73, 77 left, 78, 79; © Alan McGee/FPG, 69 left bottom; © Jonathan Stark/Heinle & Heinle Publishers, 76; Marie H. Bias, 77 right.

Unit 6: Jean Bernard, 85, 86, 87, 88, 90, 91, 92, 93, 94, 95, 96; Tsekyi Dolma, 98; Donna Carroll, 85.

Text Credits:

Unit 4: Stevie Wonder, excerpt from “Living for the City.” Copyright © 1973. Published by Jobete Music Co., Inc./Black Bull Music. Reprinted by permission of Jobete Music Co., Inc., Los Angeles, CA., 62; Lyrics from “Sixteen Tons,” copyright © Warner/Chappel, Los Angeles, CA., 63.

Unit 5: Gallup Poll, source: U.S. Immigration and Naturalization Service, 75.

COLLABORATIONS: ENGLISH IN OUR LIVES

Intermediate 2 Student Book

Jean Bernard
Donna Moss
Lynda Terrill

Heinle & Heinle Publishers
A Division of International Thomson Publishing, Inc.
Boston, MA 02116, U.S.A.

CONTENTS

*Glossary of Grammatical Terms and a List of Commo

Language Structures	Higher Order Skills and Strategies	Community Building in the Classroom
• pronoun referents • subject complements • relative clauses • preposition clusters	• previewing a reading by asking questions and reading captions • interpreting metaphors • reading graphs • reading editorials • connecting one's life experience to a text • reflective writing on the unit themes	• learning about each others accomplishments and talents • sharing ideas on maintaining cultural traditions in North America • conducting a community survey • planning a cultural event
• past perfect • past perfect continuous • root words and affixes	• previewing a reading by asking questions • paraphrasing a reading • comparing • paraphrasing idioms • identifying and using similes and metaphors • scanning for specific information • skimming for general information • connecting one's life experience to the text • reflective writing on the unit themes	• learning about each others learning strategies • comparing cultures • sharing information about educational opportunities • learning about each other's educational and employment history
• reported speech • direct quotations • advice with *should* and *ought to*	• previewing a reading by answering questions • reacting to poetry • interpreting poetry • writing poetry • identifying problems, solutions and consequences • connecting one's life experience to a text • reflective writing on the unit themes	• sharing customs of engagements and weddings • comparing cultural differences in dating and marriage • brainstorming solutions to problems
• indirect questions • forming hyphenated words	• identifying short-term and long-term goals • writing an outline for an oral presentation • making an oral presentation • using mood, rhythm to understand meaning of literature • connecting one's life experience to a text • reflective writing on the unit themes	• practicing job interview questions • sharing information about job opportunities and job skills • finding and using community resources • comparing short-term and long-term goals
• obligation with *must* and *have to* • requests with *would, could, can,* and *will*	• previewing a reading and answering questions • writing questions about a reading passage • summarizing a story • retelling a story • reading bar graphs and tables • making an oral presentation • connecting one's life experience to a text • reflective writing on the unit themes	• sharing experiences as new arrivals in North America • developing a survey • sharing results of interviews • sharing research information
• conditionals with past possibilities • conditionals with future possibilities • *wish* with past plural verbs	• previewing a reading by using visuals • sequencing chronological events • scanning for specific information • creating timelines • prewriting by note taking • connecting one's own experience with the text • reflective writing on the unit themes	• learning about other's prospects for the future • learning about major events in others' lives • sharing news from home • sharing information from a travel agency

Irregular Verbs appear on pages 103 through 105.

THE WORLD

Do you want to see where the people in this book come from? Their countries are labeled.

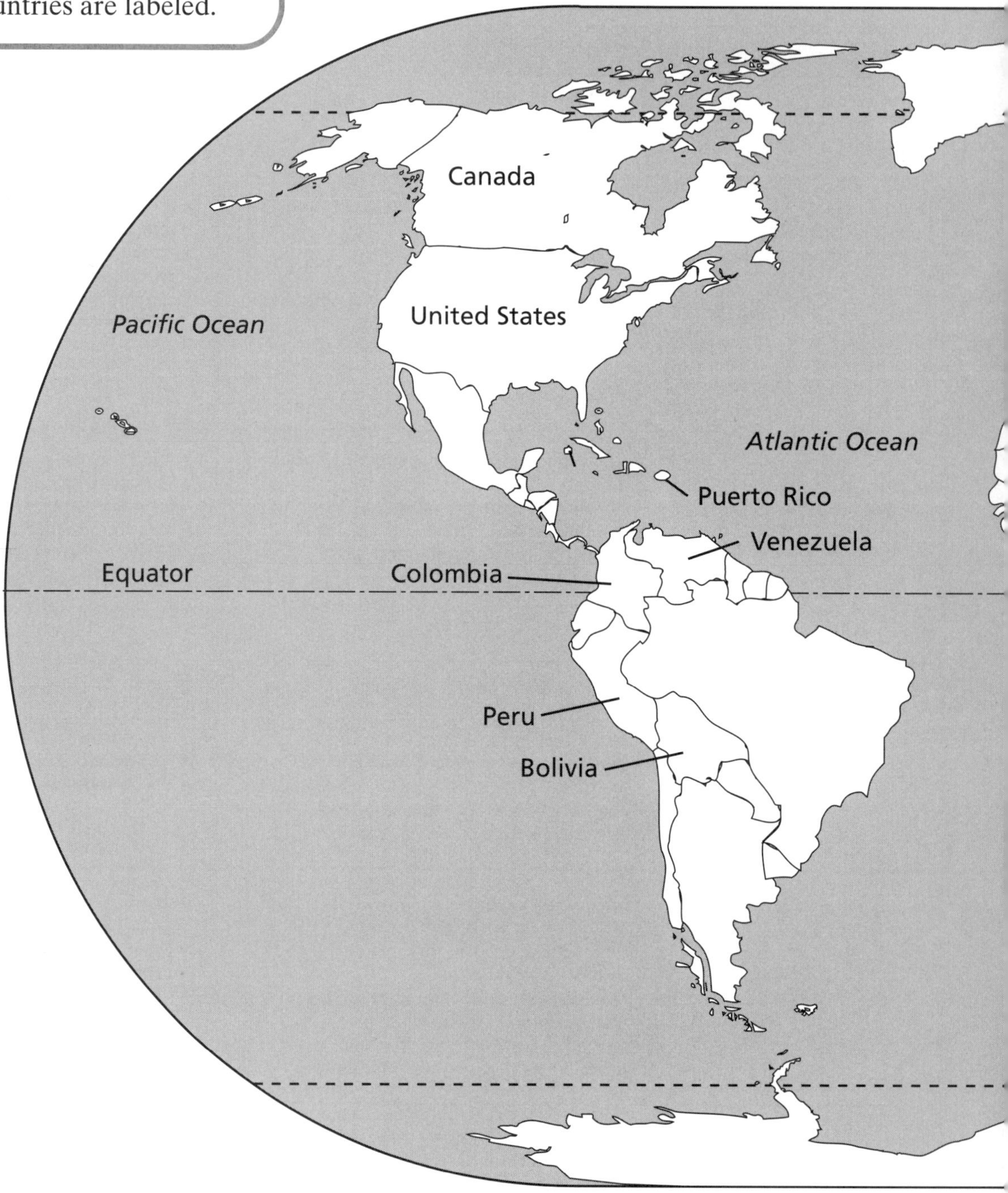

Canada
United States
Pacific Ocean
Atlantic Ocean
Puerto Rico
Venezuela
Equator
Colombia
Peru
Bolivia

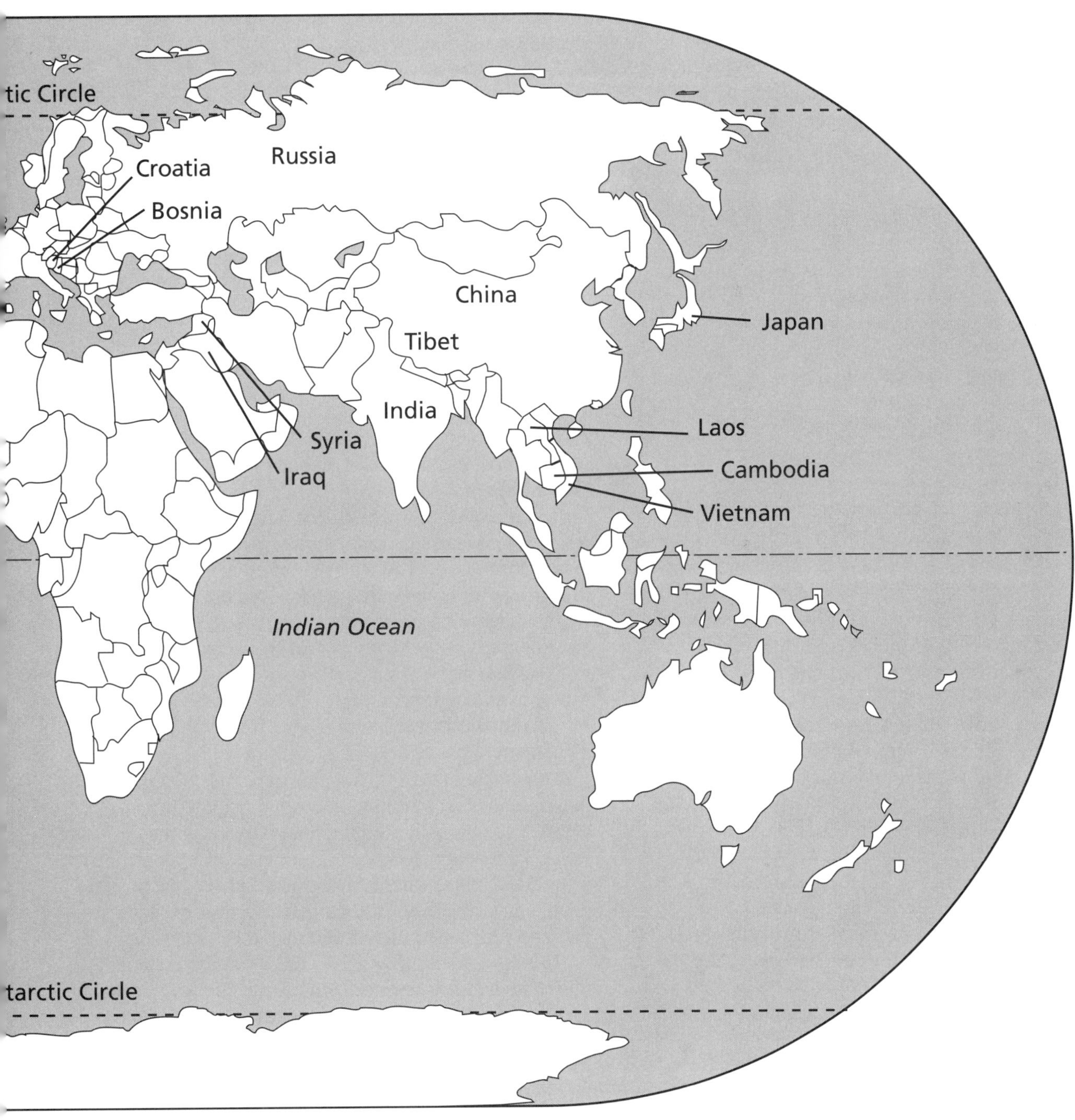
tic Circle
Croatia
Russia
Bosnia
China
Japan
Tibet
India
Laos
Syria
Cambodia
Iraq
Vietnam
Indian Ocean
tarctic Circle

ABOUT THIS SERIES

Our purpose for creating this series is to provide opportunities for adult immigrants and refugees to develop English language and literacy skills while reflecting, as individuals and with others, on their changing lives.

We believe that the best adult ESL classrooms are places where learners and teachers work collaboratively, talk about issues that matter to them, use compelling materials, and engage in tasks that reflect their life experiences and concerns. We see learning as a process in which students are encouraged to participate actively, and the classroom as a place where students share and reflect on their experiences and rehearse for new roles in the English-speaking world beyond its walls.

How are the books in the series organized?

Unlike most adult ESL materials, *Collaborations* is not organized around linguistic skills nor life skill competencies, but around contexts for language use in learners' lives. Each student book consists of six units, beginning with the individual and moving out through the series of ever-widening language environments shown below.

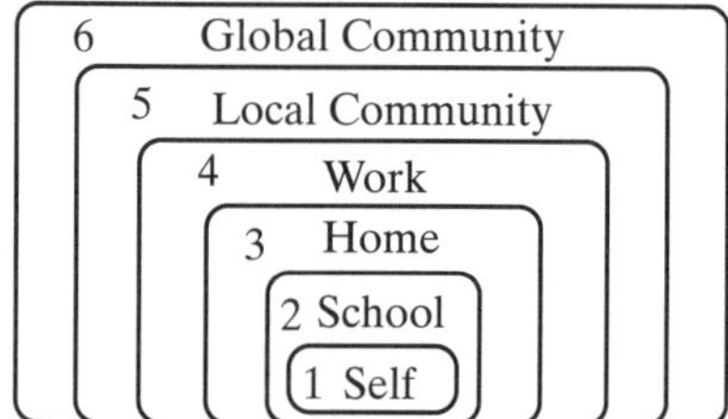

The units revolve around the narratives of newcomers who tell or write of their experiences. Each unit focuses on a particular site in North America, generally one that has a significant number of ESL programs and learners. In some locations, we have chosen a particular ethnic group. In others, we have made the multi-ethnic character of the area the focal point of the unit. It is our belief that within the marvelous diversity of newcomers, there are seeds for finding similarities—the common threads of experience—as newcomers make sense of managing life in a new setting with new constraints as well as new possibilities.

Grammar, vocabulary development, language functions, and competencies are interwoven throughout the units in each student book. However, the organizing principles are reversed from those of most traditional materials. Rather than selecting linguistic items and then creating contexts to elicit them, *Collaborations* addresses language development and competencies as they naturally emerge from the contexts and the authentic texts. For those who wish to focus more on specific competencies or language structures, detailed indexes are provided to enable participants to identify where the item is taught, and where resources for further practice can be found.

Collaborations is intended for use with learners of English in adult programs in school districts, community colleges, and community-based programs. While it is an excellent fit in non-credit programs, it may also be the right choice for some credit programs because of its strong emphasis on critical thinking and problem solving. The assessment component for the program—with its placement guidelines and instructions for portfolio assessment as well as more formal quizzes and tests—facilitates adaptation to either program. Particularly at the higher levels of the program, there is an emphasis on development of skills needed in academic programs, GED study, and workplace situations.

What are the other components of *Collaborations?*

The supplementary **workbook** for each level is correlated to the student book. It offers independent study tasks that recycle and reinforce language points from the corresponding units of the student book. Each workbook unit has a predictable structure that contains the following:

- grammar work in context
- extended reading and writing
- vocabulary work
- competency-based tasks
- tests and self assessment

In each unit, the workbook tasks follow the sequence of the activities in the student book and further develop the unit themes.

The **teacher's resource kit** consists of a variety of materials to extend classroom activities and to facilitate and assess learners' progress. The materials listed below are provided in a format that can be inserted into the teacher's kit binder.

- the teacher's edition
- wall maps of the world and of North America
- blackline activity masters
- the assessment program
- overhead transparencies
- cassette tape

The teacher's edition includes reduced student book pages, suggestions from the authors, insights from field test instructors who used the material in their classes, and space for teachers to keep their own teaching/learning journals. The transparencies are intended to be used for problem-posing activities, Language Experience writing, and oral language practice, among other things.

The assessment program includes traditional benchmarks such as pre-tests, individual unit checks, midterm and final exams, as well as guidelines for developing learner portfolios. The program is meant to encourage learners to set their own goals and monitor their own progress.

Finally, there is a cassette tape for each level. The student tape contains all the stories from each unit of the student book as well as an authentic "review interview," for which there is an accompanying worksheet in the Activity Masters in the teacher's kit.

Each unit in the student book is designed to provide at least 10 hours of activities, or 60 hours for the entire book.

However, if used in conjunction with the workbook and teacher's kit, each unit provides at least 16 hours of activities for a total of 96 hours.

ABOUT THIS LEVEL

What is included in each unit?

Each unit in this level includes:

- an introduction to the geographic area where stories in the unit are based.
- authentic narratives and photographs that have been collected from immigrant and migrant communities throughout North America. At this level, poetry, newspaper editorials, songs, folk tales, and proverbs from around the world are also included.
- multiple opportunities to react/respond to these texts and to relate them to personal experience.
- an invitation to take a closer look at the way language is used in the opening story by *Playing with Story Language*.
- guided practice in pre-GED reading and academic learning strategies in/through participation in *Think It Over* tasks, which engage learners in reacting to more formal, non-narrative writing, often accompanied by graphs, charts, or illustrations.
- one or more interactive *Learning About Each Other* tasks to foster fluency while building community among learners in the classroom.
- *Doing It in English* tasks, in which learners practice functions of English for purposes appropriate to each context.
- *Sharing Experiences* and *Sharing Ideas* activities, which invite learners to contribute their own unique perspectives on unit themes as they practice new language and critical thinking skills, such as recognizing figures of speech and identifying learning strategies.
- an invitation to *Journal Writing*, which allows students to react in writing to the themes of the unit and interact on paper with the teacher. At this level, learners are offered several options or choices of topic.
- *Other Voices from North America* which offer learners a chance to expand their reading experience by encountering a wide variety of narratives as well as other writings of varying lengths and styles.
- *Reading Strategy* and *Learning Strategy* boxes which highlight useful study strategies and bring them to conscious awareness.
- *Country Information* boxes which present informational profiles of the countries or territories represented in the unit.
- a focus on *Ideas for Action* in which learners reflect critically on their situations and decide together how they can empower themselves.
- a plan for *Bringing the Outside In*, so that learners may gain new experience and knowledge from resource people, printed materials, or realia brought in from outside the classroom.
- a list of *Options for Learning*, in which individual learners choose to study one or more communicative skills from a list of competencies (and follow up with activity worksheets).
- an opportunity to *Look Back*, where learners reflect on what they have learned, what they want to study more about, and which activities suit them the most.
- a *Checklist for Learning* to provide learners with a way to monitor their own progress and to review previous material.

QUESTIONS ABOUT *COLLABORATIONS*

The language in this book is not as controlled as other materials I've used. Will this be too difficult for my students?

Adults have been learning languages, with and without language instruction, from the time of the first human migration. Students in an English-language setting acquire language most efficiently when there is something worth communicating about. When the building blocks of language are made accessible, acquisition becomes natural and pleasurable. The aim in this series is to provide learners with the tools they need and to create conditions in which communicating is well worth the effort. Because language is a medium for negotiating social relationships, part of the goal is to create a classroom community in which English takes on meaning and purpose. The obstacles learners face because of their incomplete mastery of the English in the material are more than offset by compelling reasons to communicate.

What should I do if my students do not yet know the grammar or vocabulary in the stories and tasks?

Any teacher who has ever faced a class of eager ESL learners has had to grapple with the reality that learners come with differences in their prior exposure to English and with their own individual language-learning timetables, strategies, and abilities. There is no syllabus which will address directly and perfectly the stage of language development of any particular learner, let alone a diverse group. This material reflects the belief that learners can benefit most when forms and functions are made available in the service of authentic communicative tasks. Teaching is most effective when it taps into areas that are ready for development.

For this reason, tasks in *Collaborations* are open-ended and multi-faceted, allowing individuals to make progress according to their current stages of development. The inclusion of numerous collaborative tasks makes it possible for more capable peers as well as instructors to provide assistance to learners as they move to new stages of growth in mastering English.

It is not necessary for learners to understand every word or grammatical structure in order to respond to a story, theme, or issue. The context created by evocative photographs, by familiar situations, and by predictable tasks usually allows learners to make good guesses about meaning even when they do not control all of the vocabulary or structures they see. Any given reading or activity is successful if it evokes a reaction in the learner, and if it creates a situation in which learners are eager to respond. When appropriate language structures and vocabulary are provided toward that end, language acquisition is facilitated. Within this framework, total mastery is not critical: total engagement is.

What do I do about errors my students make?

Errors are a natural part of the language-learning process, as learners test out their hypotheses about how the new language works. Different learners benefit from varying degrees of attention to form and function. For this reason, there are supplementary activities in the workbooks and teacher's kits where learners can give focused attention to vocabulary, grammar, functions, and competencies. The detailed indexes can also assist users in locating language forms that are of immediate concern to them. Form-focused activities can be used as material for explicit study or practice, as well as for monitoring progress in language development. This series operates on the assumption that the most important ingredient for language acquisition is the opportunity to use English to communicate about things that matter. The supplementary materials will be most effective if the time set aside to focus on form is not seen as an end in and of itself, but rather, is viewed as a necessary component in developing the tools for meaningful communication and classroom community-building.

ACKNOWLEDGMENTS

This book would never have been possible without the enthusiastic help of those whose stories grace these pages. We cannot thank them all by name here, but their names appear with their stories. We are grateful to colleagues, teachers, and administrators who helped so much in arranging interviews and collecting stories, among them Laurence Aucella of Waterbury, Connecticut, the Partners, volunteers, and refugees at Jubilee Partners (Comer, Georgia), Inaam Mansoor (Arlington Education and Employment Program, Virginia), Agnes Flores (Corpus Christi Literacy Council), and Michael Westover and Judy Sides (Immigration and Refugee Services of Catholic Services, Harrisburg, Pennsylvania).

We gratefully acknowledge the originators of this series, Gail Weinstein-Shr and Jann Huizenga, as well as the other members of the original "think tank," whose ideas have continued to inspire and shape our work. We are indebted to our reviewers for their valuable insights, and to the field testers for sharing their experiences with us. We are also grateful to our mutual friend, Miriam Burt, for bringing us together.

At Heinle & Heinle, the authors are grateful to Senior Assistant Editor Sally Conover for coordinating the field testing and reviews, Caroline Boyle for her careful attention to detail, Editorial Director Roseanne Mendoza for her support and guidance through each step of the process, and Production Editor Lisa McLaughlin for her role in bringing these pages to life. We'd also like to thank Louise Gelinas and Elaine Hall at PC&F for their expert editing and production work.

We also gratefully acknowledge our sponsoring organizations, our families, and our friends for their enthusiastic and continued support. Jean's trip to Laos, during which she collected stories and photographs for Unit 6, was made possible through a grant from the Asian Cultural Council to study Lao performing arts. She would like to thank all four generations of the Dengvilay family for their incomparable hospitality, and Alysoun for her inspirational model of how to go the distance.

Donna would like to thank Robbie Buller and Chou Ly for their hospitality at Jubilee and their helpful comments on the first draft. She thanks Vlasta Zhang for her assistance as a translator with all the Bosnian families. She is grateful to her nephew Aaron Rowe for introducing her to his friends at the George Washington University. Donna also wants to thank her daughters Rachel and Laura, and her husband, David, for their patience, good humor and support.

Lynda thanks Jeanne and Dan for everything in Harrisburg. She thanks Betty for the photographs and Hung for his photography, his advice, and the gracious help of his entire family. Lynda also thanks her family for making room for the project, and she thanks her father, Hank, who was proud of her, but didn't want her to work too hard.

Finally, Donna and Lynda thank Inaam Mansoor, Suzanne Grant and the entire staff (our colleagues, friends, and students) at the Arlington Education and Employment Program for their encouragement, inspiration, and support.

Unit 1 Maintaining Cultural Traditions in Connecticut

Located in New England, Connecticut is a small state with a population of about 3,300,000. The majority of people who live and work in Connecticut were born outside of the mainland United States. Connecticut is well known for its manufacturing and service industries, where most of the newcomers to the state find jobs. The main story in this unit is from Waterbury, a major urban center with a large Puerto Rican community. Well known for its metal and rubber industries, Waterbury was once called "The Brass Capital of the World." Other major cities in Connecticut include New Haven and Hartford.

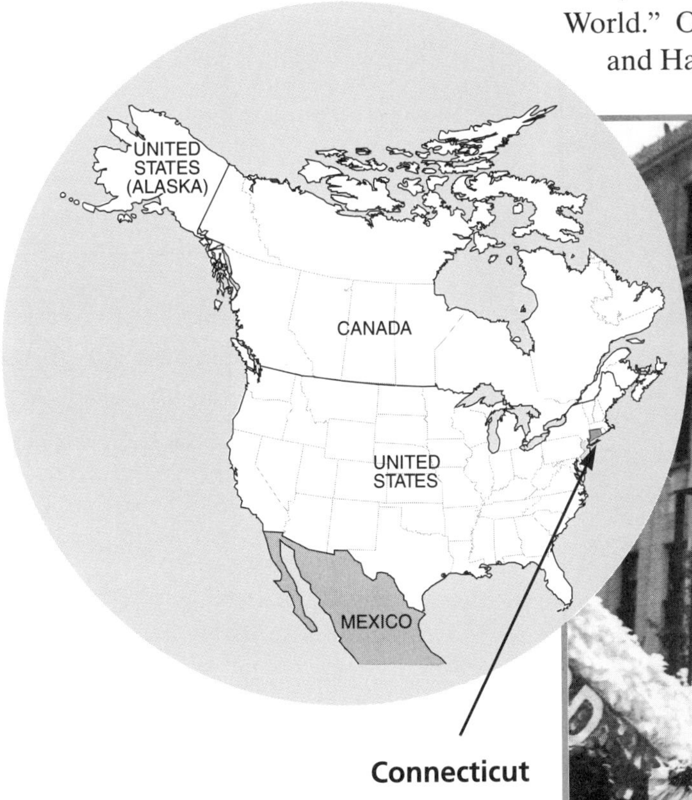

Mariano Ramos Hernandez' Story

A. Look at the photograph of Mariano Ramos Hernandez and read the caption. Where is he from? What kind of work does he do? What other things do you want to know about him? Write three questions.

Mariano Ramos Hernandez is president of the Puerto Rican Poets' Society in Waterbury, Connecticut. He has published two books, and has received many awards for his poetry. He lives in Waterbury with his wife, Alma.

B. Read the story.
Keep your questions in mind as you read.

I write about everything, but the most important thing for me is my homeland, Puerto Rico. My first poem was published when I was just eight years old. It was a very short poem called "The Tree." A couple of years later, I wrote another one for my best friend, a girl who went to school with me. It was called "Celinda." After that, every time I fell in love with a girl I wrote a poem to her.

I first left Puerto Rico in 1949. I was only a kid. I came to work on a farm in New Jersey for 50 cents an hour. Since then, I've had lots of jobs—I've been a hospital worker, a bus boy, a waiter, and a cook. I call myself a lucky guy. I always live the way you see me now—poor and humble, but happy.

IDIOMS
fall in love
only a kid
a lucky guy

I've worked hard for the last 39 years. Sometimes I had three jobs at once, but I never stopped writing poems. I used to stay up until one or two o'clock in the morning, just writing. Now that I'm retired, I have more time. They call me "El Bardo Del Vivi," (the poet of the Vivi) after a river that flows through my hometown of Utuado in central Puerto Rico. All of my poetry goes back to that place.

I am an original. I like my poetry to be understood, even by people who have no education at all, because in my poems I give a message. The only way to make that message clear is to use original words.

We Puerto Ricans are also Americans, but we want to maintain our culture here in Connecticut. We do it by speaking our language, writing books in Spanish, dancing, and organizing events like Three Kings' Day and the Puerto Rican Parade. People put out their flags and wear straw hats to show we are proud of being who we are. Our community has been doing things like this for a long time. As a matter of fact, other groups have followed our example.

How long has it been since you left your homeland?
Do you consider yourself a lucky person? Explain why or why not.
How do you maintain cultural traditions in North America?

Playing with Story Language

A. Listen to the first paragraph again. Fill in the missing words.

> _________ write about everything, but the most important thing for _________ is _________ homeland, Puerto Rico. _________ first poem was published when _________ was eight years old. It was in a Puerto Rican magazine, a very short poem called "The Tree." A couple of years later, _________ wrote another poem for _________ best friend, a girl who went to school with _________. It was called "Celinda." After that, every time _________ fell in love with a girl _________ wrote a poem to her.

B. Rewrite the same paragraph so that it is *about* Mariano Ramos. Follow the example of the first sentence.

He writes about everything, but the most important thing for him is his homeland, Puerto Rico.

____

____

____

____

C. Work with a partner. Take turns reading these parts of Mariano's story aloud. Pay special attention to the highlighted words. These words stand for other words or numbers in the same group of sentences. Write what the words stand for in the blanks to the right.

1. I first left Puerto Rico in 1949. I was only a kid. I came to work on a farm for 50 cents an hour. Since **then,** I've had lots of jobs. _________

2. They call me "El Bardo Del Vivi," after a river that flows through my hometown of Utuado in central Puerto Rico. All of my poetry goes back to **that place.** _________

3. We want to maintain our culture here in Connecticut. We do **it** _________ by speaking **our language**, writing books in Spanish, dancing, and _________ organizing events like Three Kings' Day and the Puerto Rican Parade.

Doing It in English: Describing Yourself

A. Do you remember the words Mariano Ramos Hernandez used to describe himself?

"I've been a hospital worker, a bus boy, a waiter, and a cook. I call myself a lucky guy. I've always lived the way you see me now—poor and humble, but happy."

B. Get to know three of your classmates. Find out their names and where they live. Ask what kind of jobs they have had. Then ask what words they use to describe themselves. Take notes in the chart below.

Classmate's Name	Place of Residence	Previous Jobs	Self-Description

C. Introduce one of the classmates you interviewed to the rest of the class. Use the notes from your chart.

"This is Cesar Ramirez. He lives in New Haven, Connecticut. He's been a taxi driver and a salesman. He's healthy, happy, and strong."

In this photo, Cesar is walking in the Puerto Rican parade in New Haven.

Subject Complements
After any form of the verb *be,* use a noun, a noun phrase, or an adjective.
He's always been a poet. I'm not rich, but I'm healthy and strong.

Sharing Experiences: Describing Other People

A. Read these two examples of how Mariano described other people in his story.

"I wrote another one for my best friend, a girl *who went to school with me.*"

"I like my poetry to be understood, even by people *who have no education at all.*"

B. Work with a partner. Look at the photograph. How can Ramon Vasquez identify himself in the Puerto Rican parade? Complete his description.

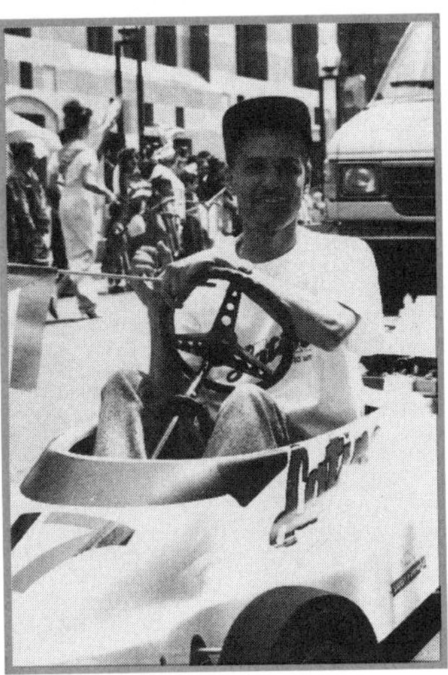

Relative Clauses with *Who*
A **relative clause** tells more about the noun it follows. When a relative clause begins with *who,* it gives more information about a person.
Mariano Ramos Hernandez is a poet who writes in both Spanish and English.

I'm the guy who ______________________________

____

C. Think of a person you know very well. Write the person's name in the center of the web diagram below.

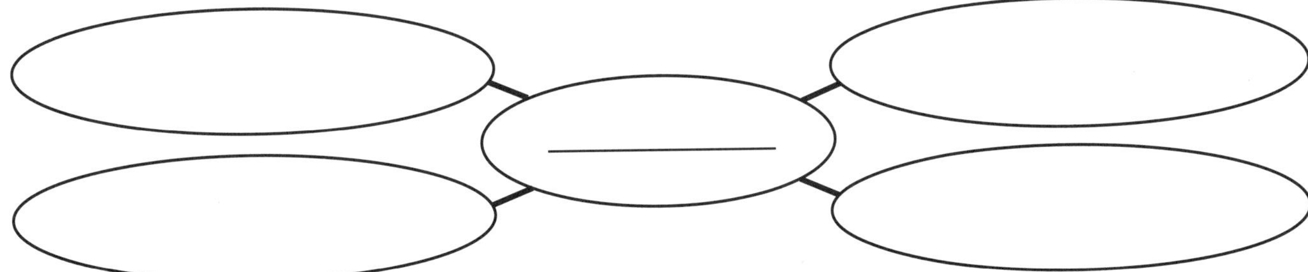

D. Complete this sentence about the person you are thinking of in as many different ways as you can.

______________ is a person who ______________________________

Write your sentence completions in the circles around the person's name on the web diagram.

E. Describe the person to a partner. Explain his or her relationship to you, then make sentences based on your web diagram.

Sharing Ideas: Reacting to Poetry

A. Read part of Mariano Ramos Hernandez' poem "Dos Patrias" (Two Lands) in Spanish or in English.

Dos Patrias

Soy un hombre
y con dos patrias
con dos nombres
dos historias
dos banderas
dos culturas diferentes
dos lenguajes
son dos patrias
dos amores

Two Lands

I am a man
with two lands
with two names
two histories
two flags
two different cultures
two languages
of two lands
two loves

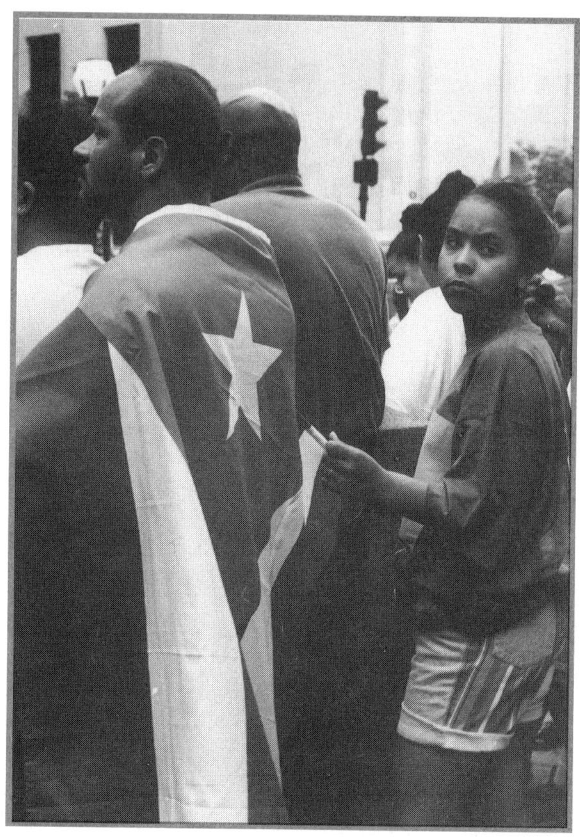

(from *Intimate Verses* by Mariano Ramos Hernandez, permission granted by the author)

B. Discuss your reaction to "Two Lands" with a partner. Use these questions as a guide.

- Do you like the poem?
- What do you like or dislike about it?
- What do you think "two loves" in the last line means?
- How does it make you feel?

C. Get together with another set of partners who have discussed the same lines. Compare your reactions.

D. Think of a few lines of a poem or song in your native language. Share them with your group, both in your native language and in English. Invite your classmates to discuss their reactions.

Learning About Each Other: Personal Accomplishments and Talents

A. Read about Mariano Ramos Hernandez' first book of poems.

> I published this collection of poetry, "Desde la Distancia," (From a Distance) in 1991. Of course, I'm very proud of it. The title means that my life is here, but my worries and my mind are in Puerto Rico. I call it that, because from a distance, it was my anguish. These are the poems I've written since I was a little boy. Some of them are the stories my mother taught me. All of the poems in this book are in Spanish, but I do write poems in English sometimes.

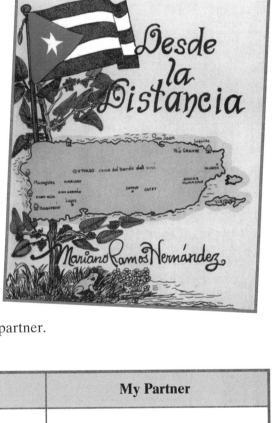

B. Discuss these questions with a partner.

- What special ability does Mariano Ramos have?
- How has he used this ability?

C. A *talent* is a special ability to do something, such as write poetry, dance, or play music An *accomplishment* is anything you have done that you are proud of. What are your talents? What have you accomplished in your life so far? Tell a partner. Take notes in the chart.

	Me	My Partner
Talents		
Accomplishments		

D. Tell the class about your partner's accomplishments and talents.

Learning About Each Other: Things We're Proud Of

A. Discuss the event in this photograph with a partner. Why do you think the people in this community are celebrating? What are they proud of?

B. Explain something you are proud of or happy about to a small group of your classmates.

Using Preposition Clusters

An adjective is often used with a preposition following a form of the verb *be*. Together, the adjective + preposition are called a **preposition cluster.** After a preposition cluster such as *proud of, happy about, sure of,* you can use (a) a noun, (b) a gerund phrase, or (c) a noun clause beginning with *what* or *who.*

Mariano is **proud of** { his poetry / working hard / who he is }

I'm happy about my new job. What about you?

I'm proud of being Puerto Rican.

Puerto Rico is an island in the Caribbean Sea, east of Haiti and the Dominican Republic. The population of Puerto Rico is 3,522,520, and the capital is San Juan. Puerto Rico was a colony of Spain until 1898, when it became a possession of the United States as a result of the Spanish-American War. Puerto Ricans were granted U.S. citizenship in 1917, and the Commonwealth of Puerto Rico was established in 1952. Since the turn of the century, over 2.5 million Puerto Ricans have migrated to Hawaii, New York City, and the New England states to work at various jobs in agriculture and industry.

8 Sharing Experiences: Cultural Traditions in North America

A. Discuss ways the people in these photographs are maintaining traditions from their native lands.

B. How do you maintain cultural traditions in North America? Share your experiences and ideas.

C. Do you think it is important to maintain traditions from your native land in North America? Check (✔) the statement that you agree with most. Explain your opinion to your group.

It's not very important to me. ❑

It's somewhat important to me. ❑

It's very important to me. ❑

9 Think It Over: Is America a Melting Pot?

A. Look at the cartoon. What do you think it means? Talk it over with a partner. Then read the explanation of the term, "Melting Pot" in the box below.

"The Melting Pot" is the name of a play about immigrants written by Israel Zangwill. In the play, which opened in Washington, D.C. in 1908, one of the characters declared:

"America is . . . the great Melting Pot where all the races of Europe are melting and reforming . . . Germans and Frenchmen, Irishmen and Englishmen, Jews and Russians—into the Crucible with you all! God is making the American!"

Although very few Americans living today have seen Zangwill's play, the term "melting pot" is still widely used and discussed. Basically, it is a metaphor* for becoming a new person in a new land. People who support the melting pot idea believe that newcomers should "become American" as quickly as possible. That is, they should speak only English, wear baseball caps, and eat apple pie.

*metaphor—a word or phrase used to stand for something different than its usual meaning. A metaphor is one type of figure of speech.

Reading Strategy

Cartoons, drawings, and photographs are different types of illustrations. Illustrations help readers understand the meaning of new ideas.

B. Reread the last sentence in the box. Have you "become American" in these ways? With your partner, brainstorm some of the other ways newcomers change when they come to America.

______________________, ______________________, ______________________

Learning Strategy

Listen and read for the ways metaphors are used in English. Ask teachers or friends to help you clarify the meanings of these terms.

C. Here are two other metaphors people sometimes use to represent ways people of different cultures and languages live together in North America. Work with your partner to invent a third metaphor of your own. Share it with the class.

Melting Pot,
Salad Bowl,
Patchwork Quilt,

____

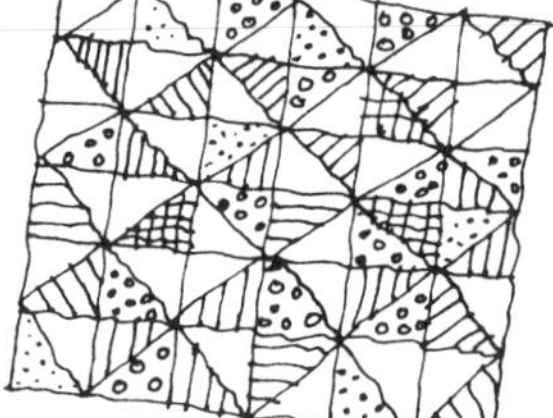

10 Doing It in English: Expressing and Recording Opinions

A. Should languages other than English be used in your ESL classroom? Check (✔) your opinion:

1. English only ❑

2. English most of the time ❑

3. Not sure ❑

B. Discuss your opinion with a small group of classmates. If you checked "English most of the time," explain exactly when using other languages might be helpful. If you checked "Not sure," explain what questions or doubts you have.

C. Count the different opinions in your group and report to the class. Then complete the report below for the whole class.

OPINION SURVEY

Number of students who . . .

1. support "English only" ________

2. support "English plus*" ________

3. are not sure ________

*English and one or more other languages

D. The graph below shows the results of a similar opinion survey in a large North American city that has a large French-speaking population. Use the information in the graph to complete the sentences below.

Should the street signs in our city be in both English and French?

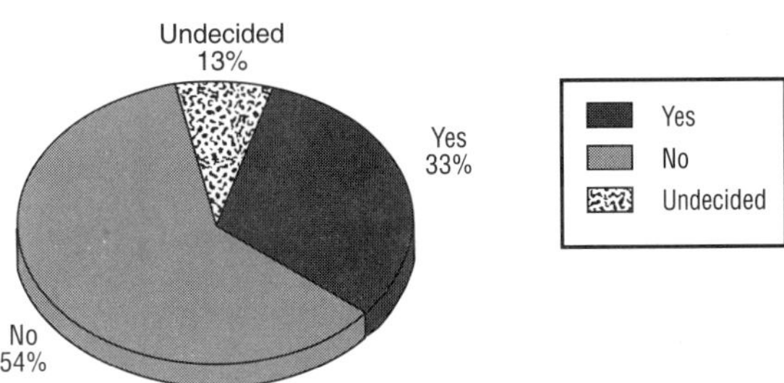

1. The majority of people surveyed felt that ________________________________.

2. ____________ of those asked said that the new signs should be in both English and French.

3. ________________________________ had not made up their minds.

E. Work with a partner. Based on the results of your class survey, draw lines and label the sections of the graph below. Then write three sentences that describe your graph.

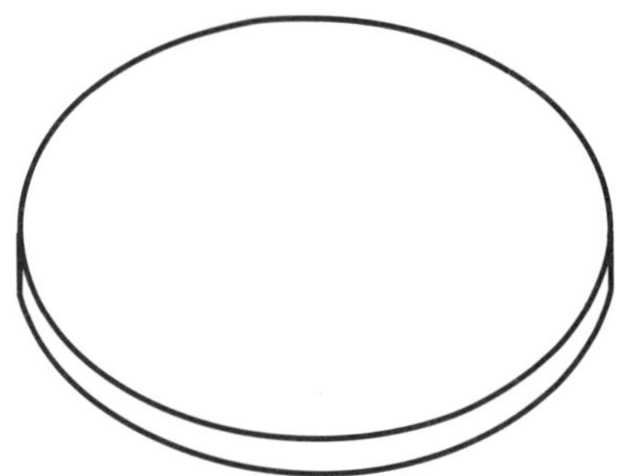

F. How do you feel about the role of English in your life outside the classroom? Read over the list below. Which of these things should people living in North America be able to do only in English? Which things should they be able to do in their first languages or in English?

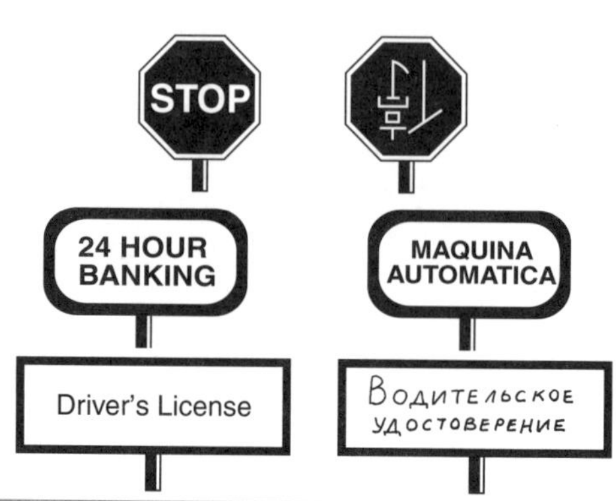

	English Only	English Plus (English or Native Language)
Open a bank account.	❑	❑
Get a job.	❑	❑
Take a driver's license exam.	❑	❑
Participate in religious services.	❑	❑
Get medical help.	❑	❑
Get information about government programs.	❑	❑
Become a citizen of the U.S. or Canada.	❑	❑
(other) ______________________	❑	❑
______________________	❑	❑

G. Tell your group which items on the list you checked and explain why.

Journal Writing: People and Ideas

In your journal, describe yourself or someone you know very well. These are some things you might want to include:

- where you come from
- where you live and work now
- some things you have done
- some things you are proud of

Write more about *your* experience in this country. Explain why you are learning English, and what your goals are. Give examples of where it is important to use English, and in what situations you prefer to communicate in your native language.

12 Other Voices from North America

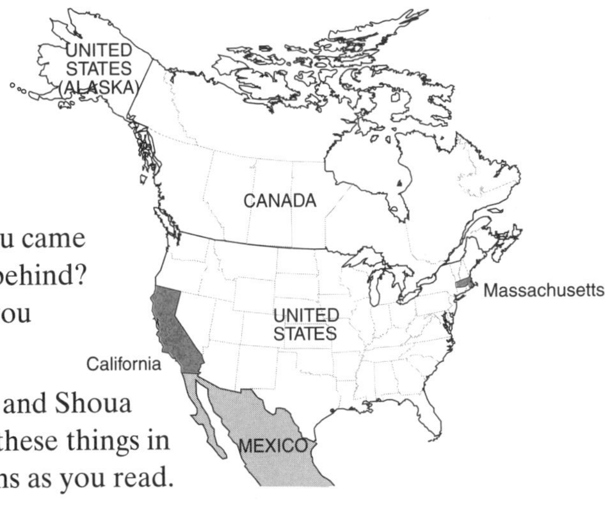

A. What things did you bring with you when you came to this country? What things did you leave behind? Share some examples with the class before you read the stories.

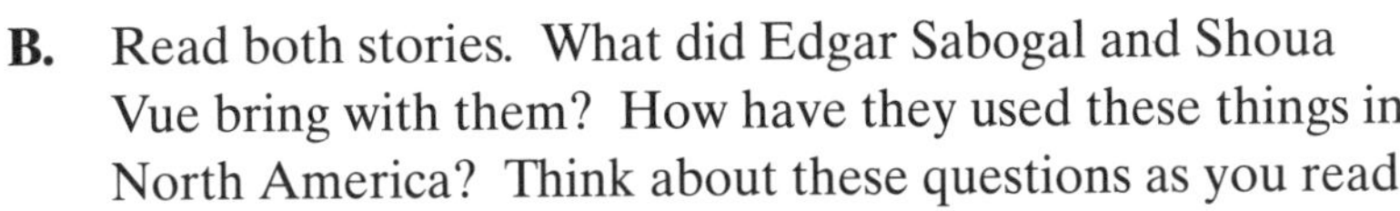

B. Read both stories. What did Edgar Sabogal and Shoua Vue bring with them? How have they used these things in North America? Think about these questions as you read.

C. Circle the words you want to remember.

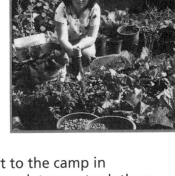

I see a lot of emptiness in North American cities. In New England, the cities are colder, and the colors are dull and gray. People are isolated from each other. They are crowded together into small spaces, but they don't communicate.

When I look at a city, I have this kind of reaction. Something inside of me is warm, maybe because I am from a place that is close to the Equator, where the sun is directly overhead. As a child, I was used to seeing green any time of day. So now, when I paint a city here in New England, I add the colors.

Sometimes when North Americans look at my paintings, they are shocked because I have a different way of looking at cities. Bright colors like purple, green, and orange are too confusing for some people. I just want people to see my work. I want to say to them, "These are my colors!"

Edgar Sabogal is a fine artist who works in Holyoke, Massachusetts. He is originally from Colombia.

We left Laos with all those seeds and plants that are good for healing. We carried them in the boat crossing the Mekong River and planted them again when we got to the camp in Thailand. Three years later we took them with us to America. They are precious to us. Our forefathers had brought them when they moved from China to Laos over a hundred years ago. Here in San Diego some of the plants grow better than others, but between my mother and me, we haven't lost any yet.

I also use Tylenol® and Anacin®, and sometimes Contac®, but not often. Our medicine is different. It makes the body strong. We use it inside and outside. I grow about ten different kinds. Some taste very good, and I put them into chicken soup.

Shoua Vue is a member of the Hmong minority group from Laos. She lives with her family in San Diego, California.

13 Doing It in English: Reading Newspaper Editorials

A. In an *editorial,* the writer expresses an opinion about a certain topic. The editorial below appeared in a newspaper in Hartford, the capital of Connecticut. Read the editorial, then decide whether you agree or disagree with the writer's main point.

Reading Strategy
As you read, look for the main point. Consider the examples and reasons the writer uses to support his or her opinion.

A Lesson from My American Grandmother

by John Andrews

My elderly grandmother, who arrived in this country from Scotland in 1922, was recently in an automobile accident. At the hospital, the doctors who were treating her could not understand a word of the strange language she was speaking. They thought she had gone crazy. Just then, a nurse who had recently immigrated from Scotland arrived at her bedside, stopped for a moment to listen to the familiar sounds. The nurse reported to the doctors that there was nothing at all wrong with the old lady's brain. She was not off her rocker. She had simply gone back to Gaelic, the language of her early childhood.

I can't help but think sometimes that the supporters of the English-as-a-national-language movement are just as shortsighted as the doctors who treated my grandmother. As the children and grandchildren of immigrants ourselves, we must never forget that languages other than English are part of our heritage, too. Speaking another language should not make anyone strange, different, or less American.

IDIOMS
off her rocker
the American dream
wall of fear

As a matter of fact, what we love best about America—the promise of freedom and the chance for a better life—are the very same values our most recent immigrants cherish. The Iranian grocer, the Somali taxi driver, the Bosnian refugee all share this hope. Many of these newcomers have been through much more hardship than any of us can even imagine. The fact that they may not yet speak perfect English has nothing to do with their loyalty to their new homeland, or to their willingness to work hard to achieve the American dream.

The desire of our new immigrants to keep cultural traditions alive does not conflict with their desire to become Americans. According to the principle of religious freedom, upon which this country was founded, there is no reason why a Cambodian temple, a Russian church, or a Moroccan mosque, should not be warmly welcomed here. Likewise, when we think of freedom of speech, we must not insist that immigrants abandon their native languages as they learn English. We must instead get rid of the wall of fear that arises from the fact that many of us do not speak other languages. We must learn to celebrate differences as we learn more about each other. As my grandmother would say, we will be richer for it.

B. Check the sentence that best expresses the writer's main point.

- ☐ The doctors had never heard my grandmother's native language before.
- ☐ Immigrants should try harder to be like other Americans.
- ☐ New Americans should feel free to maintain their languages and cultural traditions.

C. Do you agree or disagree with the writer's main point? Explain your reasons to a partner.

14 Bringing the Outside In: Conducting a Community Survey

Take your own survey of opinions in your local community. Ask several of your teachers, friends, or family members about the importance of maintaining cultural traditions in North America.

With the class, decide on the questions you want to ask. Work with a partner to conduct short interviews. Bring the results to class. With the help of your teacher, you may present the results in the form of a chart.

These are the questions one class wrote:

How do you maintain cultural traditions in North America?
Where do you communicate mainly in English?
Where do you communicate mainly in your native language?
Do you agree with "English only" or "English plus?"

15 Ideas for Action: Planning a Cultural Event

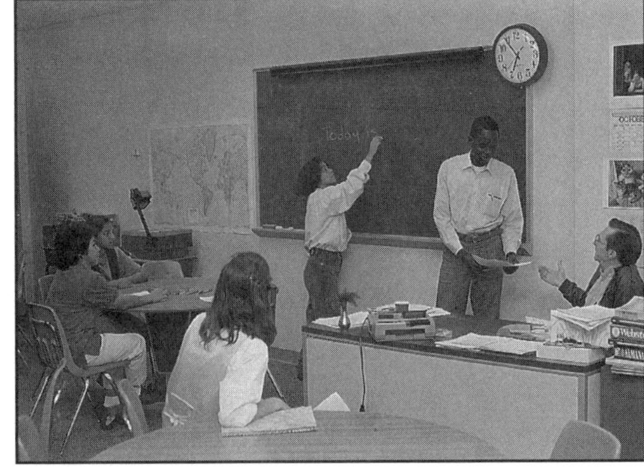

A. Plan a cultural event in which you and your classmates demonstrate ways of maintaining cultural traditions. Your plan need not be complicated or expensive. Work with a small group to work out the details. Include these steps in your planning.

1. Decide on a time and date.
2. Decide who you want to invite.
3. Plan how you will advertise the event.
4. Put together a program. Decide what each person in your group will do. (examples: read a poem, share some food, demonstrate a custom)
5. Estimate how much the event will cost and suggest ways of paying for it.

B. Present your group's plan to the whole class. When all the plans have been presented, vote on the best plan for your situation.

C. With your teacher's help, decide as a class if you actually want to carry out the plan. If everyone agrees it is a good idea, decide what the next steps should be.

Options for Learning: Communicating About Cultural Traditions

A. What do you want to tell people about yourself or your culture? Check (✔) your answers. Add other ideas if you wish.

	Already Do	Want to Learn	Not Interested
Locate information about your country or culture.	______	______	______
Explain a cultural tradition or custom.	______	______	______
Write a letter to a newspaper expressing your opinion.	______	______	______
Form an organization for maintaining your language and culture.	______	______	______
Other? ______________	______	______	______

Looking Back

Think about your learning. Complete this form. Then tell the class your ideas.

A. The most useful thing I learned in this unit was ______________________________

____.

B. I would still like to learn ______________________________.

C. I learned the most by working

______ alone. ______ with a partner. ______ with a group.

D. The activity I liked best was 1 2 3 4 5 6 7 8 9 10 11 12 13 14 15 16

because ______________________________.

E. The activity I liked least was 1 2 3 4 5 6 7 8 9 10 11 12 13 14 15 16

because ______________________________.

Checklist for Learning

I. Vocabulary: Add more words and phrases to each list. Check(✔) the ones you want to remember. For extra practice, write sentences with the new words and phrases.

Words to Describe People

_____ lucky
_____ humble
_____ ________________
_____ ________________
_____ ________________
_____ ________________
_____ ________________
_____ ________________

IDIOMS

_____ a lucky guy
_____ ________________
_____ ________________

Occupations

_____ waiter
_____ busboy
_____ ________________
_____ ________________
_____ ________________
_____ ________________
_____ ________________
_____ ________________

Personal Talents

_____ sing
_____ dance
_____ ________________
_____ ________________
_____ ________________
_____ ________________
_____ ________________

Ways of Maintaining Cultural Traditions

_____ speaking native languages
_____ writing poetry
_____ ________________
_____ ________________
_____ ________________
_____ ________________
_____ ________________

II. Language: Check (✔) what you can do in English. Add more ideas if you wish.

I can

_____ describe myself or a person I know well
_____ recognize words that stand for times, places, and things in a reading passage
_____ explain something you are proud of or happy about
_____ read and discuss a poem
_____ talk about your personal talents and accomplishments
_____ recognize and interpret metaphors
_____ ask for, express, and discuss personal opinions
_____ ________________________________
_____ ________________________________

III. Listening: Listen to the Review Interview at the end of Unit 1. Ask your teacher for the *Collaborations* worksheet.

Unit 2 Sharing Strategies in Harrisburg, Pennsylvania

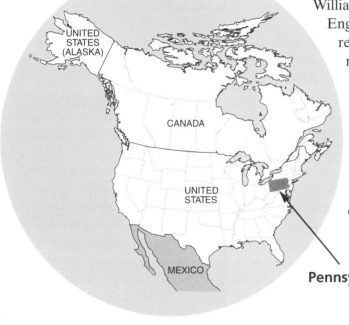

The first stories in this chapter come from Harrisburg, the capital of Pennsylvania. Pennsylvania was founded in 1681 by William Penn on land given to him by King Charles II of England in payment of a debt. In part because of Penn's religious beliefs, the colony quickly became a haven for religious dissenters and other immigrants. Immigrants have come to Pennsylvania from many parts of Europe through the 300 years of its history. Now people emigrate to Harrisburg from Russia, Vietnam, Iraq, Ethiopia, and many other places. They learn English and North American culture, and they learn to study together at programs such as those run by the Immigration and Refugee Services of Catholic Charities of Harrisburg.

Four Stories from Harrisburg

A. What are some effective ways to learn English? How can people learn and teach at the same time? Are your goals similar to others' in your class? Compare your ideas.

B. As you read the stories, compare the philosophies and goals of these people with those of your classmates, instructors, and yourself.

Iraq contains the fertile valleys of the Tigris and Euphrates rivers where Mesopotamia once flourished. About 97 percent of Iraq's 21 million people are Muslims. Under the rule of Saddam Hussein, the war with Iran and the 1991 Gulf War have caused terrible damage to the people and the country of Iraq.

Ali shares his ideas in one of Michael's classes at Immigration and Refugee Services of Catholic Charities.

Ali Al-Shermery's Story

I am from Basra, Iraq. I came here six months ago. I have a job, and I always come to school. I am a carpet installer. I was an Arabic teacher in Iraq. In 1991, I was part of the uprising against Saddam Hussein. Later, I couldn't live in my country, and I moved to Saudi Arabia. I came here in 1994. Two days a week I study English. Speaking is easiest for me. I'm not good, but, you know, I'm trying. So, sometimes I can't read, sometimes I can't write, but I can speak. I don't need a translator. If I don't speak English, I won't eat. I've only studied English here. I listen to music, I watch T.V., and I listen to different people. I listen to different dialects. I have to understand. After five years, if Saddam Hussein dies, I will go back to my home again. I think I want to be a teacher for kids, or maybe, I will be a businessman.

Michael studied many languages. Now he wants to help his community.

Michael Westover's Story

IDIOMS
main thrust
in the same boat
wakes them up

I was born in Augusta, Georgia. I've lived in Harrisburg since 1981, and I've been a teacher with Catholic Charities since 1991. I have one class in the morning that prepares people to work, and the main thing I want them to be able to do at work is to speak to co-workers and their bosses. I think if they can do that, they can learn everything else on the job. I think the main thrust in my night class is to make people from different cultures work together peaceably. We talk about the differences in religions. In the evening, I have Catholics, Muslims, and Jews all together. I make them talk about the similarities and the differences and help them to respect their differences and enjoy their similarities. I do the same thing with education and social status. I show them that they are in the same boat when it comes to English and that they have to help each other and that really wakes them up.

Learning Strategy

In a good dictionary you can find definitions, grammar, idioms, pronunciation, and the history of words.

Izrail Dubrovitsky's Story

I was an electrical engineer in Russia. I had that job for 47 years. Now I have no job; I am a pensioner. The people in the United States are very friendly to people who come from other countries. I study here for two hours, four days a week. In my country, I had learned German. Before I came to the United States, I studied English for just two months. Because I come from another country, I have many problems, and I need many documents. The official papers come to my mailbox, and I have to answer them. At first, when I came to the United States, I needed to look at every word in my dictionary. I translated the sentences with my dictionary. I needed to translate many times because I couldn't understand which definitions were proper for me. At home, I watch T.V., but I don't understand the way people are talking. I want to have more conversations with native speakers.

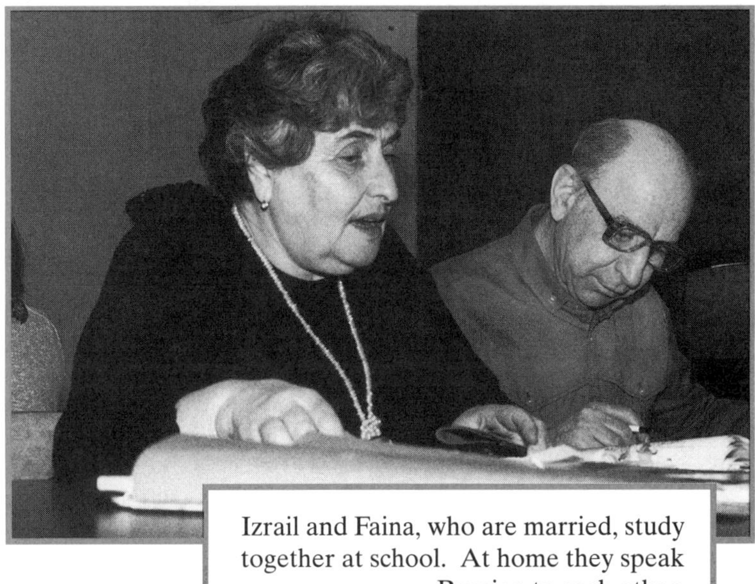

Izrail and Faina, who are married, study together at school. At home they speak Russian to each other.

Russia is the largest country in the world. It covers 11 of the world's time zones. Between 1922 and 1991, Russia was the most powerful republic of the Soviet Union. Now, Russia is in a period of political, social, and economic change.

Faina Belkina's Story

For 40 years I was a neurologist in Russia. Now, life is difficult for me. I read books. I read better now, but I don't understand conversation well. I also watch TV. The conversation on TV is very fast, and sometimes I don't understand the situation. In class, we do reading one day, grammar another day, and we also use the dictionary. Studying in the class is very good. My progress in reading and writing is better than in conversation.

I live in a very big building with many neighbors. With a very nice neighbor, we celebrate many American holidays. At home, I do homework, I read, and I watch TV.

2 Playing with the Story Language

A. Restating a text in your own words, or paraphrasing, is one way to make sure you understand the essential meaning of a text. Choose one of the Harrisburg stories and reread it. When you understand the story, tell it to a partner. Do you both agree about the content of the story?

Original Text	Paraphrase
I need to go into a different life than my life before. (Izrail)	My life changed. I have to change.
Now people travel to Harrisburg from Russia, Vietnam, Iraq, Ethiopia, and many other places.	People come to Harrisburg from many places.

IDIOM
in your own words

B. Now, below, use simple, clear sentences to paraphrase the story:

____

____

____

____

____

____

____

____

____

____

C. In his story, Michael Westover uses two common idioms: "they are in the same boat" and "that really wakes them up." Using the story itself to give you clues, paraphrase the idioms. Share your ideas with your partner. Do you agree or disagree about the meaning of the idioms? Do you have similar idioms in your native language?

1. ____

2. ____

3 Learning About Each Other: Life Before North America

Izrail said that he needed more English so he could begin a different life than the one he had had before. He had been working as an electrical engineer in Moscow for 47 years. Israil's wife, Faina, had been a neurologist for 40 years before they left Russia.

A. Ask some of your classmates about their lives before they came to North America. Record the answers on the chart. Compare the answers. Do you see any similarities?

Name	How many years did you go to school?	What did you study?	Had you studied English before you came here?	What was your job before?

B. Identify the verb tenses in the paragraph at the top of the page and in the chart that you filled out. Why do you think past time can be expressed in so many ways? What ways do you use to express past time? Share your ideas with the class.

Past Perfect
Ali had taught Arabic before he moved to Saudi Arabia.
The past perfect tense shows action that finished before another action in the past. This tense is formed by adding **had +** the **past participle** to the subject.

Past Perfect Continuous
Michael had been living in Harrisburg before he began teaching.
The past perfect continuous tense shows action that continued for some amount of time before another action in the past. This tense is formed by adding **had + been +** the **present participle** to the subject.

4 Doing It in English: Explaining What We Need

Adriana Ariza had studied microbiology in Colombia before she came to the United States. In her country she had been working in quality control in food. Adriana says she needs to speak English. She studies in Michael Westover's class at Immigration and Refugee Services in Harrisburg, Pennsylvania.

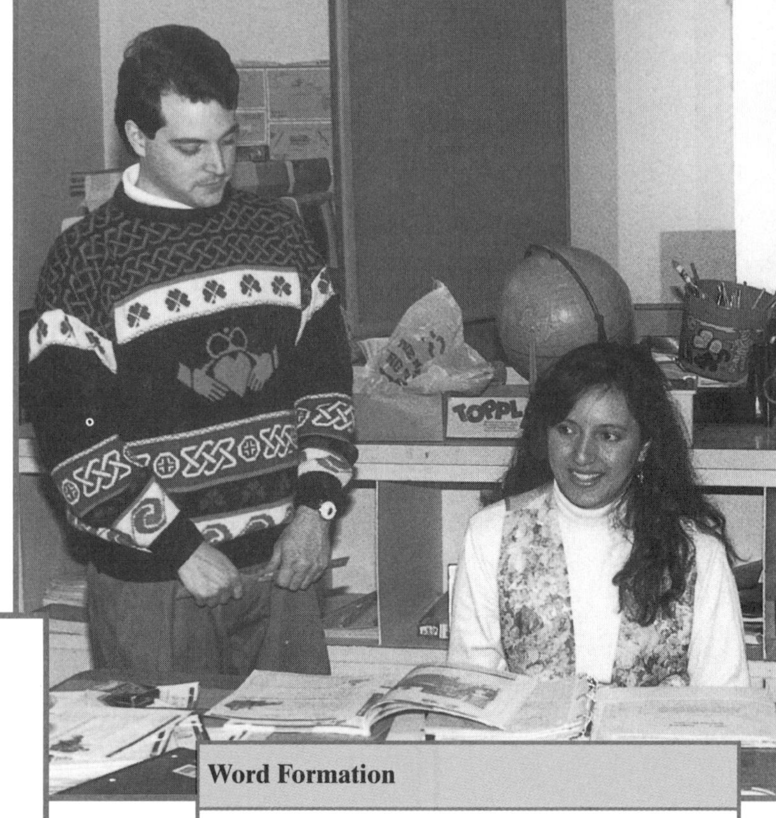

In English there are many ways to express necessity:

I need a job.
I need to work.
I have to study.
I must practice every day.
I've got to speak more.
It's necessary to listen carefully.

Word Formation

I **need** to study.
It's **necessary** to go.
Practice is a **necessity**.

To understand the meaning and the function of words, look at the **roots** and the **affixes**.

A. Why do you need to study English? Work with a small group to write a list of reasons why it is necessary to study English. Share your list with the whole class. Does each group list the same reasons?

____

____

____

____

____

____

____

Other Voices from North America

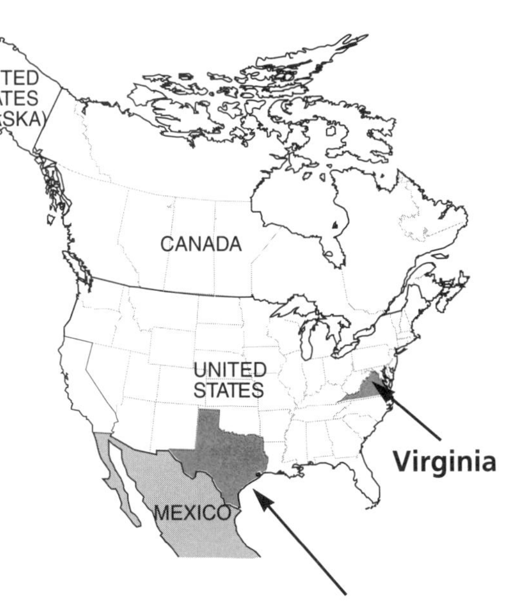

A. Think about your school now and before you came to North America. What was the relationship between students and teachers? Do you have that same relationship with your teachers now?

B. Read the story. Keep your questions in mind as you read.

Thu-Thuy Nguyen came to the United States from Vietnam. She studies at Northern Virginia Community College. She lives with her family in Arlington, Virginia.

In some ways teachers are both the same and different than in Vietnam. I can tell you about the differences. In my country, when I was a small child, my father always taught me. So, in Vietnam, teachers are like parents. You have respect for them. In this country it is different because the students go to the school and, after they finish, some of them forget about their teachers. In my country that's not the custom. When I was small, I studied in middle school and I have always remembered that. So, the teacher always keeps the relationship with the students—all of them. The teacher is always proud of them and always helps them if they have difficulties in their lives.

Before I came here, listening to English was very difficult. After that, I went to school and to work and it was very easy to practice speaking and listening. I have a problem and I think other students are like me. They have some problems with reading. You know, sometimes when you read *The Washington Post* or *The New York Times,* you can not read all the words—you always find new words. So I think this is my weakness. I think right now I have to learn new words. When I find a new word, I write it down in a notebook, and I find it in the dictionary. After that, I make a sentence. Also, I have read short stories and after that, I have read novels, because the college always requires students to take English. It's not English As a Second Language and, for the class, you have to read books. So I try to read every day. Right now I am reading *Animal Farm.*

PROVERB
English: First learn politeness, then learn knowledge.
Vietnamese: Tiên học lễ, hậu học văn

Moustafa Kattih is from Syria. He lives in Corpus Christi, Texas. In the future he would like to teach in a university here in the United States. Moustafa studies at the Corpus Christi Literacy Council.

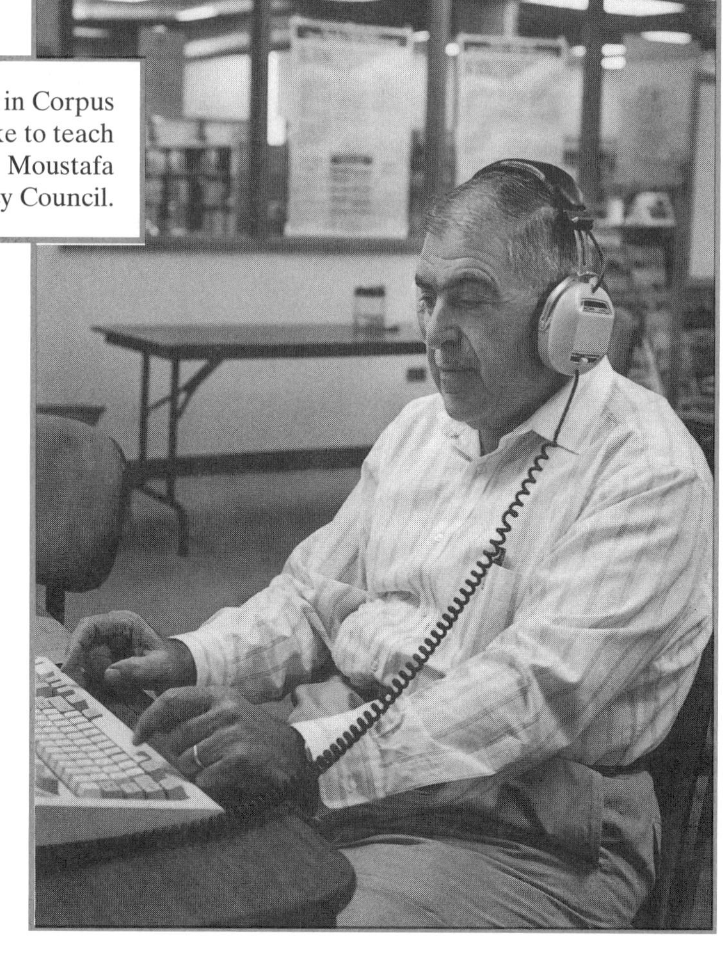

I was a teacher in the high school and college. I taught Arabic literature. I taught about 30 years and then I retired, and I came here to visit my son.

A teacher is a prophet because he makes the human being. Every job makes things: this man sells something, this man makes an electrical machine, this one builds homes, but we build the person. So, in my religion, the best person in the world is one who teaches others because he builds the person. This is from Prophet Mohammed. The soldier kills, the construction worker builds a roof; but in all the world, the teacher is the best person.

The second thing, in all the world, we really love the students. Parents love their kids more than themselves and the teachers love their students more than themselves. The teachers always are very tired because they give from their hearts and not from their arms. I will tell you one sentence: If I went back in my life 40 years, and I was back in high school in 1952, I wouldn't study anything different—only to be a teacher another time.

Vietnam lies along the South China Sea in Southeast Asia. The Vietnamese people make up approximately 90 percent of the population, but there are many minority groups such as the Chinese, Khmer, Muong, Meo, and Thai. Hundreds of thousands of people died in the Vietnam War, and many thousands emigrated.

Syria is at the eastern edge of the Mediterranean Sea. The capital, Damascus, is over 4,000 years old. Syria has been important throughout its history because it lies along trade routes that link Asia, Africa, and Europe. Most of Syria's more than 15 million people are Muslim Arabs.

Think It Over: The Culture of Education

A. In their stories, Thu-Thuy and Moustafa expressed strong beliefs about students, teachers, and learning. Both used special kinds of language to express intense feeling. Special types of language, such as **metaphors** and **similes,** are called **figures of speech.** Find and list figures of speech from each story. Check your ideas with the class.

Figures of Speech
Alliteration Metaphor Overstatement Paradox Personification Simile Understatement

Similes
Learning English is like making vegetable soup.
Similes compare two unlike things using the words **like** or **as.**

Thu-Thuy:

____

____

Moustafa:

____

____

B. Think about your own culture. How do people think about students, teachers, and learning? Finish the following phrases with figures of speech or words from your culture.

Teachers are (like) ______________________________.

Children (or students) are (like) ______________________________.

School (or education) is (like) ______________________________.

C. Compare your sentences with your group and then with the whole class. Are the sentences similar or different? On the computer or using poster board and markers, write the sentences in English and in your native language. Find a place to share your ideas: the entrance to your school, the office, a bulletin board, or maybe an elementary school!

7 Doing It in English: Identifying and Suggesting Learning Strategies

A. The students in this unit have written about methods, or strategies, which help them to learn English. List at least three strategies from the stories.

Strategies
The student's strategy was to read the newspaper every day.
A strategy is a specific plan to accomplish a particular goal.

Student	**Strategy**
____________	____________________
____________	____________________
____________	____________________
____________	____________________

B. Do you use any of the above strategies to learn English? Are they effective? Work with your group to brainstorm a complete list of language learning strategies. Try to decide which strategies are most effective for the most students. When you have the final list, ask your teacher which strategy he/she thinks is best. Do you agree or disagree?

____

____

____

____

____

____

____

PROVERB
English: A book is a friend.
Vietnamese: Sách là một người bạn.

Bringing the Outside In: Movies

A. Watch the movie, *Stand and Deliver,* with your classmates and teacher. Work with a partner to answer the following questions and then talk with the class about the movie.

1. What is happening in the movie?

____

2. Who are the characters in the movie?

____

3. What is the setting of the movie (where/when is it)?

____

4. What is the main idea of the movie?

____

5. What emotions are expressed in the movie?

____

6. Is the movie easy or difficult for you to understand? Explain.

____

B. Is watching a movie a good strategy for learning English? Why or why not? Discuss your answers with the whole class.

C. Work with the class to recommend a list of movies, TV shows, and radio programs that might help students practice English skills.

Journal Writing: Students and Teachers

Choose one of the following topics to write about:

1. Compare your experiences studying English with those of one of the students you've read about. Have your experiences been similar or not? Explain your ideas.

2. Think about teachers here and in your native country. What are the essential characteristics of a good teacher? Explain your ideas.

Reading About It: Skimming and Scanning for Information

Reading Strategy: Skimming
Reading titles, headings, introductions and summaries, and bold words can help you understand the general meaning of an article quickly.

Reading Strategy: Scanning
Letting your eyes quickly move over the text can help you find specific information that you need, such as: numbers, dates, names, or places.

A. After noting the titles and subtitles of the following article, quickly skim it. Write the main idea of the article in two or three sentences.

____

____

____

____

B. Compare your sentence with your classmates' sentences. Do you agree or disagree about the main idea of the article?

CORPUS CHRISTI LITERACY COUNCIL PROGRAMS
"OPEN WINDOWS TO THE WORLD"

The Corpus Christi Literacy Council is located at 4044 Greenwood with office space in the Greenwood Library. Regular office hours are 8:00 A.M. to 5:00 P.M., Monday through Friday.

ONE-ON-ONE TUTORS

Volunteers are trained and certified in a sixteen (16) hour Workshop conducted by certified Tutor Trainers to teach adult students to speak, read, and write the English language. Upon certification, tutors are assigned to students, seventeen years of age or older, reading below a fifth grade competency level or who do not speak the English Language.

The majority of tutoring sessions are conducted at public tutoring sites. There are sixty-nine (69) locations within the Corpus Christi City limits as well as in the Corpus Christi Literacy Council's headquarters. CCLC continues to solicit and train an average of one hundred thirty-five (135) tutors each year to be matched with students in an effort to help with the tremendous need.

Individuals interested in receiving literacy assistance are evaluated by the CCLC to determine current reading level and the ability to speak English conversationally. After the initial evaluation, an application is filed until the individual can be matched with a certified tutor.

The only requirements for a participant are that he/she does not speak English or speaks English in a limited capacity, reads on or below a fifth grade level, is not enrolled in a public school, and is at least seventeen (17) years of age.

TUTOR TRAINING

The Corpus Christi Literacy Council provides Tutor Training to local groups and agencies as well as neighboring cities who request training.

Volunteers are trained and certified in a sixteen (16) hour Workshop conducted by qualified Tutor Trainers. Upon certification, tutors are able to teach students to speak, read, and write the English language.

A person interested in becoming a tutor must be seventeen (17) years of age or older and attend a certification workshop. For more information contact CCLC at 857-5896.

PROJECT-ADVANCE

Project Advance is a classroom instruction program that teaches adult basic literacy instruction. Students attend classes twice a week for six months or approximately 100 hours of instruction. Class sessions are held January through June and July through December. Approximately twenty (20) students are served in each session.

The goal of this program is to enable the participants to increase their reading and writing skills to about a fifth grade competency level. Upon reaching this goal, students are referred to higher level education agencies.

MICROREAD

The MicroRead program is conducted through a partnership grant funded with Job Training Partnership monies. This program is conducted at Del Mar College West Campus and the C.C. Literacy Council classroom. MicroRead is a mixture of computer-assisted and classroom instruction. Depending on the current year's funds, 60 to 100 participants are served each year.

Components of the program include ESL, math, basic literacy, and occupational skills enhancement activities. Participants who qualify for JTPA assistance and are language barriered, nonreaders, and/or reading below a 7.0 grade level are eligible for this program.

Participants are enrolled for forty-seven (47) weeks receiving 100 hours of computer-assisted instruction, 100 of literacy and math instruction combined, and 24 hours of occupational skills training.

C. Quickly scan the article again to answer the following questions:

1. What are the office hours of the Corpus Christi Literacy Council?

   ____

2. How many volunteers does the CCLV train every year?

   ____

3. What is the minimum age to be a tutor?

   ____

4. How many students are served each session in PROJECT-ADVANCE?

   ____

5. How many hours of computer-assisted instruction are MicroRead participants offered?

   ____

Ideas for Action: Educational Opportunities in the Community

A. Find information about educational opportunities in your area. Work with your class to make a chart or bulletin board. Include information about times, places, cost, and requirements.

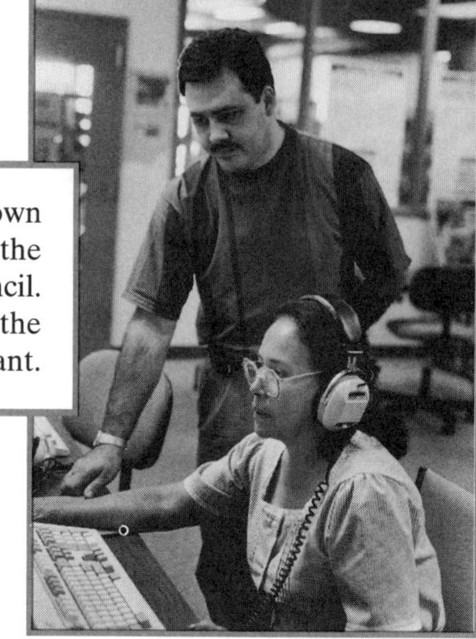

Although Humberto Gonzales runs his own company, he finds time to teach at the Corpus Christi Literacy Council. Humberto believes that respecting the adult learner is necessary and important.

PROVERB
English: To learn is a gift from God, but to teach is a calling.
Spanish: Aprender es un don, pero enseñar es un apostolado.

B. Interview one of your classmates or someone outside the class. Ask the following questions, plus one of your own. Compare the answers with the rest of the class.

Describe your favorite teacher (in the past or now). Explain the reasons why this teacher is special.

____

____

What qualities make a good teacher? Why?

____

____

What responsibilities for learning belong with the teacher and with the learner?

____

____

____

Your question: ________________________________

____

____

Options for Learning: Using Strategies Outside Class

A. What strategies do you want to use for studying English outside of class? Check (✔) your answers. Add others if you wish.

	Already Do	Want to Do	Not Interested
Find a conversation partner to practice speaking and listening.	______	______	______
Volunteer in the community to practice language skills.	______	______	______
Read the newspaper every day.	______	______	______
Write in a journal every day.	______	______	______
Other? ____________	______	______	______

Looking Back

Think about your learning. Complete this form. Then tell the class your ideas.

A. The most useful thing I learned in this unit was ______________________________

____.

B. I would still like to learn ______________________________.

C. I learned the most by working

_______ alone. _______ with a partner. _______ with a group.

D. The activity I liked best was 1 2 3 4 5 6 7 8 9 10 11 12

because ______________________________.

E. The activity I liked least was 1 2 3 4 5 6 7 8 9 10 11 12

because ______________________________.

Checklist for Learning

I. Vocabulary: Add more words and phrases to each list. Check (✔) the ones you want to remember. For extra practice, write sentences with the new words and phrases.

Ways to Learn

_____ compare
_____ paraphrase
_____ __________
_____ __________
_____ __________
_____ __________

Describing Learning and Teaching

_____ similar
_____ effective
_____ __________
_____ __________
_____ __________
_____ __________

IDIOMS

_____ in the same boat
_____ __________
_____ __________

Ideas

_____ strategy
_____ respect
_____ __________
_____ __________
_____ __________

Figures of Speech

_____ simile
_____ __________

PROVERB

_____ A book is a friend.
_____ __________

II. Language: Check (✔) what you can do in English. Add more ideas if you wish.

I can

_____ Explain what I need
_____ Compare and contrast ideas
    _____ in writing
    _____ in conversation
_____ Identify my own/others' language learning strategies
_____ Suggest strategies for learning English
_____ Paraphrase a story
_____ Scan a text for specific information
_____ Skim a text for general meaning
_____ Understand and use figures of speech for emphasis
_____ __________
_____ __________

III. Listening: Listen to the Review Interview at the end of Unit 2. Ask your teacher for the *Collaborations* worksheet.

Dating and Marriage in Washington, D.C.

Washington, D.C. is the capital of the United States. In 1790 Congress gave permission for a site on the Potomac River to be chosen for a new capital city. Maryland and Virginia gave land for the city. This area was centrally located in what was then the United States. The capital was named the District of Columbia after Christopher Columbus and the city was called Washington to honor George Washington, the first president of the United States. People from all over the country and all over the world go there to study, work, and live. Millions of tourists come every year to visit the Capitol, the White House, and Washington's famous monuments and museums.

UNITED STATES (ALASKA)
CANADA
UNITED STATES
MEXICO
Washington, D.C.

Sandeep Bagla and Monisha Sehgal's Stories

A. What do you know about American dating and marriage customs? How are American dating and marriage customs different and similar to customs in your country?

B. Read the stories. Compare marriage and dating customs of India to your country.

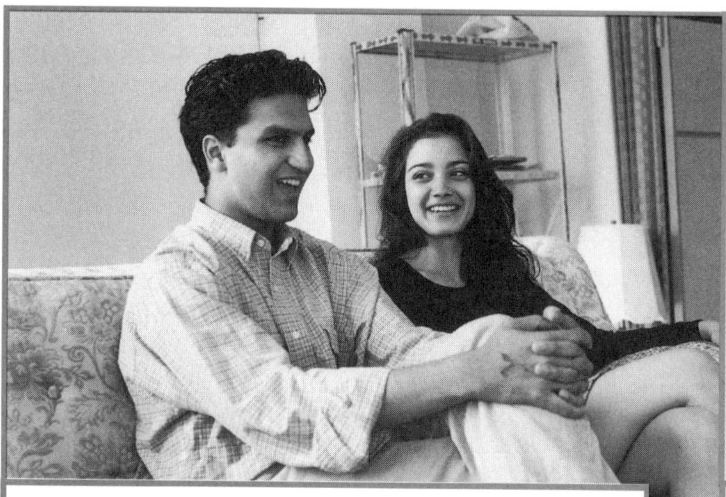

India is the second most populous country in the world with 937,000,000 people. It has about 24 major languages including Hindi, which is the primary language. India has a rich ancient culture dating back 4,000 years. It is the birthplace of Hinduism and Buddhism, two of the world's great religions.

Sandeep Bagla was born in New York. His parents emigrated to the United States from India. Monisha Sehgal was born in California and has lived in the United States, Italy, and India where her parents are from. They are students at George Washington University in Washington, D.C.

IDIOMS
paved the way
go out on dates
find out
catch on
give in
play the field

Sandeep Bagla:

My parents are originally from northern India but I grew up in New York. I have two older sisters and they spent their first five to eight years in India. Then my family moved here. My parents were raised in India and they instilled in us their values on dating and marriage. In a sense my sisters paved the way for me because my parents are more liberal with me.

My oldest sister was never allowed to go out on dates because when my parents first came here they were very strict. My other sister wanted to go out on dates and my parents tried to be a little more open with her. Then I started dating, but when I was in the ninth grade they found out I was seeing a girl who was two years older than me. They hated this and they forbade me to see her anymore.

For the next two years I didn't talk to my parents. I would come home from school, eat dinner, go to my room to do school work and then go to bed. It was horrible because we didn't have a relationship for two years. After two years they began to give in a little and I also gave in. They realized that for me and my friends, dating did not mean marriage.

During those two years they had a lot of opportunities to talk to their friends about what their kids were doing so they were slowly catching on to what dating meant here. At the same time, I quietly accepted more of their ideas.

I see now that dating should not take away from anything else. Education is my main goal. Dating is more of a serious thing for me and I think my relationships have been more serious than many of my friends' relationships.

Even though my parents are more open, they still would not be happy if I just went out on casual dates with lots of girls. In other words, playing the field is not acceptable. So we both changed. Five years ago when I asked my parents if I could go out on a date my mother said no. When I asked her if she knew what a date was, she said no and she didn't want to know. Now they are more accepting and I can talk to them about Monisha. Now they are more interested in what I did on a date than the fact that I went on a date. You know how kids want their parents to be their friends? Well, it is becoming more like that.

> If you were in Sandeep's situation what would you have done?
> If you were Sandeep's parent, what would you have done?

Monisha Sehgal:

> **IDIOMS**
> casual flings

If I were raised in the area of India where my parents are from, I would not be dating. If I did date, it would be to the person I was going to marry. There would be no other person. My cousins who live in India don't even think about dating and their marriages are arranged. They always ask me about dating customs here. They tell me that they think it is so weird that people can have several boyfriends or girlfriends before they get married.

In India girls start getting proposals somewhere between the ages of 16 and 18, depending on the family. Usually by the time a girl is 20 she knows when she will get married. The guys are generally three or four years older than the girls, so that they are established in work and settled.

My parents have already received proposals for me. They don't say much to me because they are liberal that way, but they do think that I should be looking forward to marriage instead of just having casual flings with different boys.

Compared to many of my friends who are completely American, I refrain from just dating anyone. I am looking for a long term commitment but many of my friends are not that serious. They say that they are still in college and they don't have to worry about it. They say that they have the rest of their lives to think about marriage.

> Monisha is looking for a long term commitment but her friends are not as serious. Who do you agree with?

Playing with the Story

A. Listen to part of Sandeep's story. Write the missing words.

Even though my ________________ are more open, they still ________________ not be happy if I just ________________ out on casual dates ________________ lots of girls. In other ________________, playing the field is not acceptable. So we both changed. Five years ago when I ________________ my parents if I could go ________________ on a date my mother ________________ no. When I asked her if she ________________ what a date was, she said no and she ________________ want to know. Now they are more ________________ and I can talk to them ________________ Monisha. Now they are more ________________ in what I did on a date ________________ the fact that I went on a date. You know how kids want their ________________ to be their friends? Well, it is ________________ more like that.

Reported Speech	
Quote He said, "I **need** to study English." She said, "I **wrote** a letter."	Reported Speech He said he **needed** to study English. She said that she **had written** a letter.
Reported speech tells what someone said without using a direct quote. **Direct quotes** in the simple past or present perfect can be changed to past perfect in reported speech.	

B. Underline the sentences with reported speech in each story.

C. Change the reported speech to direct quotes from Monisha's story.

1. They tell me that they think it is so weird that people can have several boyfriends or girlfriends before they get married.

   They told me, "We think it is so weird that people can have several boyfriends or girlfriends before they get married."

2. They say that they are still in college and they don't have to worry about it.

   ____

3. They say that they have the rest of their lives to think about marriage.

   ____

Learning About Each Other: Finding a Mate

A. Learn about a classmate's country. Complete the first part of the table about your country. Then, interview your partner about marriage and dating customs in their country.

	Your country	Your partner's country
1. How do couples become acquainted?		
2. Do people date?		
3. At what age do men and women begin dating?		
4. Where do people go on dates?		
5. At what age do people usually get married?		
6. Is it acceptable for a man or a woman to stay single?		
7. Are marriages arranged?		

Expressing Generalities	
Generally, men ask women for a date. **Usually,** men ask women for a date.	Men **generally** ask women for a date. Men **usually** ask women for a date.
Generally and *usually* can be placed at the beginning of the sentence or before the verb.	
In general, men ask women for a date.	**As a rule** men ask women for a date.
As a rule and *in general* also express a typical occurrence.	

B. Write sentences about your partner's country that express generalities about dating and marriage. Show your partner.

____

____

____

____

Another Story from Washington, D.C.: An Interview with the Almanzas

Dorothy and Marcos Almanza live in the Washington D.C. area. Dorothy is from the United States and teaches English as a second language. Marcos is from Bolivia and is a construction worker.

A. How easy or difficult do you think it would be to have a bilingual or bicultural relationship? Do you know couples who come from different cultures or have different first languages?

B. Read the story. Circle the words you want to remember.

Dorothy

I think language plays a big part when we are spending time with his family. I know very little Quechua and Spanish. I try to understand the conversation and I understand a little but I don't want Marcos to feel he has to translate all the time. That can interfere with the time he is spending with his family.

Marcos

Sometimes language plays a role in our relationship. For example, when she is having a conversation with someone about books they are reading, I can't always get into the conversation. I didn't grow up in this culture and I didn't read any of these books so it can be kind of hard to participate in the conversation. When that happens I just slip out.

IDIOMS
play a role
a little bit
slip out
spend time with
get a point across

Dorothy

When we are having an argument sometimes it gets frustrating trying to get our points across. We might start an argument and then realize we weren't really disagreeing at all because we were just having some little misunderstanding about language. After talking for a while, one of us will say something like, "Oh, that's what you meant!"

I think we are a lot more patient with each other than in the beginning. Now we recognize that many of the differences that we used to see as being cultural differences are just the way we are as people. Sometimes in the beginning we would say to ourselves "Oh that's cultural." We would use it as an excuse. We don't do that anymore. Now we try to work things out instead of using that excuse.

Bolivia is located in the central part of South America. The population of Bolivia is almost 8,000,000. About one third of the country lies more than a mile above sea level in the Andes Mountains. From the Andes the land stretches to the Amazon lowlands. Bolivia is a landlocked country. It shares control of Lake Titicaca, the highest navigable lake in the world, with Peru.

C. Discuss the following questions with a small group.

1. How do language and cultural differences play a role in the Almanza's relationship?
2. Have you ever had a misunderstanding or funny experience because you didn't understand someone's language or culture or someone didn't understand yours?

5 Journal Writing

Choose one of the following to write about in your journal.

1. Describe a conflict that you had with your parents. What was it about? How was it resolved?
2. Tell about a date you or someone you know had.
3. Tell about a misunderstanding you or someone you know had because of language.

Sharing Ideas: The Perfect Mate

Sincerity is really important. Also flexibility—the ability to adapt is important.

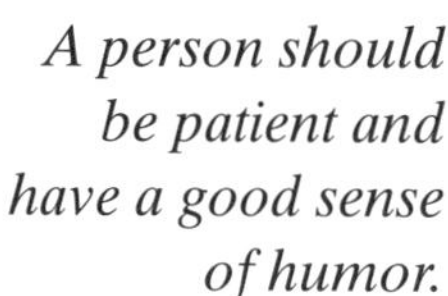

A person should be patient and have a good sense of humor.

A person should be a good companion and somebody you can trust. She's told me her closest secrets and I've told her mine. I never think twice that it's going to go anywhere afterwards.

They should be someone you can talk to and someone who is always there for you.

A. In a small group look at the following characteristics. Put a check ✔ on those that are very important to you or your partners.

The perfect mate should:	You	______ (name)	______ (name)	______ (name)
1. have a good education	______	______	______	______
2. have a lot of money	______	______	______	______
3. have a sense of humor	______	______	______	______
4. be patient	______	______	______	______
5. be handsome or beautiful	______	______	______	______
6. have a good job	______	______	______	______
7. be from my culture	______	______	______	______
8. be flexible	______	______	______	______
9. be trustworthy	______	______	______	______
10. know how to cook	______	______	______	______
11. ______________	______	______	______	______
12. ______________	______	______	______	______
13. ______________	______	______	______	______
14. ______________	______	______	______	______

Learning Strategy
By sharing ideas we expand our knowledge and awareness of differing opinions.

B. Share your information with the rest of the class. In general, what were the most important characteristics?

____

____

____

____

7 Doing It in English: Making, Accepting, and Declining Invitations

Write in the calendar below three things you have to do this week. Next, begin inviting your classmates to participate in an activity with you. If your classmate **can** join you, add the name and activity to your calendar. Fill the entire week with activities.

Sunday	**Monday**	**Tuesday**	**Wednesday**	**Thursday**	**Friday**	**Saturday**
A.M.:	A.M.:	A.M.:	A.M.:	A.M.:	A.M.:	A.M.:
P.M.:	P.M.:	P.M.:	P.M.:	P.M.:	P.M.:	P.M.:

Making and Responding to Invitations	
Do you want + infinitive: Would you be interested in + gerund:	Do you want **to do** something tomorrow? Would you be interested in **going** to the movies?
Accepting an invitation:	I'd like that. That sounds nice.
Declining an invitation	I'd love to, but . . . I'm afraid I can't because . . . *It is considered polite to give an explanation.*

8 Bringing the Outside In: Wedding Ceremonies

Teach the class about your country. Bring in photos or traditional symbols of an engagement or wedding from your country. Share them with the class.

An engagement is a period of time that begins when two people decide to get married. Often the man gives the woman a diamond ring as a symbol of their engagement. During this time they plan their wedding. The bride usually wears a white dress and veil. The groom wears a formal suit called a tuxedo. The couple chooses two people to be witnesses of the marriage—the maid of honor and the best man. The wedding is usually followed by a party called a reception. One tradition is for the bride and groom to cut the wedding cake and feed each other a piece.

Alan Geralnick and Adrienne Eng are from the United States. They were married in Brooklyn, New York.

This wedding took place in Hartford, Connecticut. The couple had a traditional Lao Buddhist ceremony after a Western ceremony in a church.

9 Doing It in English: Reading and Writing Poetry

A. Read the poem and discuss the questions.

THE NIGHT HAS A THOUSAND EYES

The night has a thousand eyes,
And the day but one;
Yet the light of the bright world dies
With the dying sun.

The mind has a thousand eyes,
The heart but one;
Yet the light of the whole life dies
When love is done.

Francis William Bourdillon

Francis William Bourdillon was a British poet. He lived from 1852 to 1921.

1. What do the thousand eyes of the night represent?
2. What do the thousand eyes of the mind represent?
3. How does the poem make you feel?
4. Why do you think the poet wrote this poem?

Learning Strategy

Interpreting is explaining what something means to you. Individuals may not have the same interpretation of a poem. When you share your interpretation, give reasons for your ideas.

Reading Strategy

Poetry often uses images to communicate ideas and feelings. As a reader, use these feelings to help you interpret the poet's message.

B. What images do you see when you read this poem? Draw a picture of the poem. Share it with the class.

C. A *cinquain* is a five-line poem. The cinquains on this page have a grammatical structure. Each line needs a specific type of word.

Line 1 = 1 NOUN
Line 2 = 2 ADJECTIVES
Line 3 = 3 VERBS with *ing* endings
Line 4 = 1 COMPLETE SENTENCE
Line 5 = 1 NOUN (different from the first)

Chiyo Yasuda studies English at the Garnet Adult Center in Charleston, West Virginia.

Family
warm, close
gathering, trusting, loving
Family is the smallest, tightest group of people.
Dinner
Chiyo Yasuda

Friend
funny, smart
loving, sharing, caring
Life is sweet with you at my side.
Dave
Donna Moss

Donna is one of the authors of this book. She teaches English in Arlington, Virginia. David is a computer specialist in Washington, D.C.

D. Brainstorm with the class possible topics for a cinquain.

E. Write a cinquain. Share it with the class.

____

____

____

____

____

10 Think It Over: Finding Solutions

In a small group read and discuss **one** of the following situations. What are the problems? What advice would you give to the people? What might happen if they follow your advice? Report your ideas to the class.

1. Ana is from El Salvador but lives and works in Toronto. Ana's daughter, Elisa, is seventeen years old. Elisa met a young man named Alfredo in her chemistry class in high school. Alfredo has asked her to go to the movies on Friday night. Ana tells her daughter she can not go because Ana does not know Alfredo or his family. Elisa is angry and tells her mother that all her friends go on dates and that she is not a baby. She says that she will find a way to go out with Alfredo.

2. Hung and Ginny are getting married. Hung is from Vietnam and wants to have a traditional Vietnamese wedding. Ginny is from the United States. She wants a small civil wedding with only the immediate family members attending. She wants to save the money for their honeymoon.

3. Ali and Rachida are from Morocco. They are living in the United States. Ali studies at the university and Rachida lives with her parents and works in a bank. They are in love and plan to get married. Ali wants to return to Morocco when he graduates. He wants to start a business. Rachida loves her work in the United States and wants to remain in the United States close to her family.

Learning Strategy
Ask youself what consequences a solution to a problem might have.

Problems

____

____

Solutions	Consequences
____________________	____________________
____________________	____________________

Advice with *should* and *ought to*	
She **should call** the doctor.	He **ought to practice** English everyday.
Should and **ought to** are used to express advice. They are followed by the simple form of the verb.	

Options for Learning: English at Home

A. What tasks do you want to perform in English? Check (✔) your answers. Add other tasks if you wish.

	Can Do	Want to Learn	Not Interested
Write an invitation.	____	____	____
Read more poetry.	____	____	____
Learn lyrics to a romantic song.	____	____	____
Call for information about movie schedules	____	____	____
Other? ____________	____	____	____
____________	____	____	____

12 Looking Back

Think about you have learned in this unit. Complete the form. Then tell the class your ideas.

A. The most useful thing I learned in this unit was ______________________

____.

B. I would still like to learn ______________________________.

C. I learned the most by working

________ alone. ________ with a partner. ________ with a group.

D. The activity I liked best was 1 2 3 4 5 6 7 8 9 10 11

because ______________________________________.

E. The activity I liked least was 1 2 3 4 5 6 7 8 9 10 11

because ______________________________________.

Learning Log

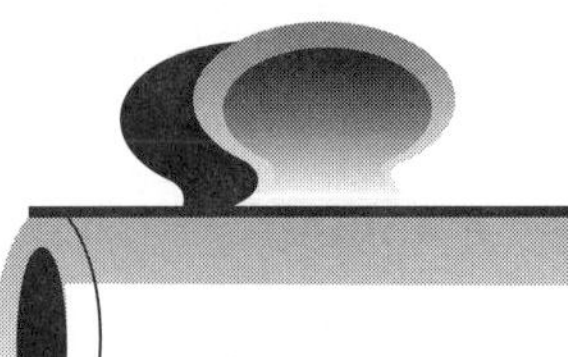

Checklist for Learning

I. Vocabulary: Add more words and phrases to each list. Check (✔) the ones you want to remember. For extra practice, write sentences with the new words and phrases.

Words to Describe Relationships

_____ dating
_____ a fling
_____ ____________________
_____ ____________________
_____ ____________________
_____ ____________________
_____ ____________________

Wedding Nouns

_____ bride
_____ groom
_____ ____________________
_____ ____________________
_____ ____________________
_____ ____________________
_____ ____________________

Describing Characteristics

_____ a sense of humor
_____ trustworthy
_____ ____________________
_____ ____________________
_____ ____________________
_____ ____________________
_____ ____________________

IDIOMS

_____ go out
_____ catch on
_____ ____________________
_____ ____________________
_____ ____________________
_____ ____________________

II. Language: Check (✔) what you can do in English. Add more ideas if you wish.

I can

_____ identify problems and solutions
_____ ask for and express personal opinions
_____ read a poem
_____ explain interpretation of a poem
_____ write a poem
_____ describe a custom or tradition
_____ express generalities
_____ give, accept and decline an invitation
_____ ____
_____ ____

III. Listening: Listen to the Review Interview at the end of Unit 3. Ask your teacher for the *Collaborations* worksheet.

Unit 4 Finding Success in Corpus Christi, Texas

The first story in this unit comes from Corpus Christi, Texas. Corpus Christi is a port city on the Gulf of Mexico. The name of the city reflects the bicultural history of Texas. Although the first inhabitants of Texas were Native Americans, the first Europeans to explore the region were the Spanish in 1519. Texas was a part of Mexico until 1836. In Corpus Christi, many people work in chemical refineries, and many people still make a living from the sea. Many immigrants still come to Texas from Mexico and other parts of Latin America, but others come from all parts of the world seeking and finding success.

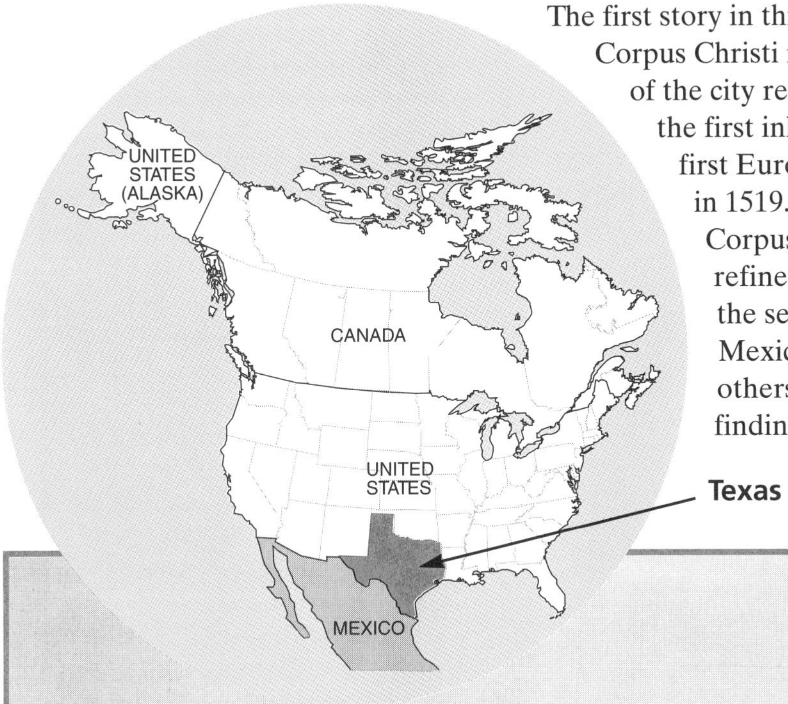

Maria Munoz's Story

A. Maria Munoz was born in San Diego, Texas. She has worked hard all of her life. When you read her story, notice her attitudes about work, learning, and life in general. Compare her experiences and her attitudes with your own.

B. As you read the story, think about what questions you would ask Maria if you could meet her.

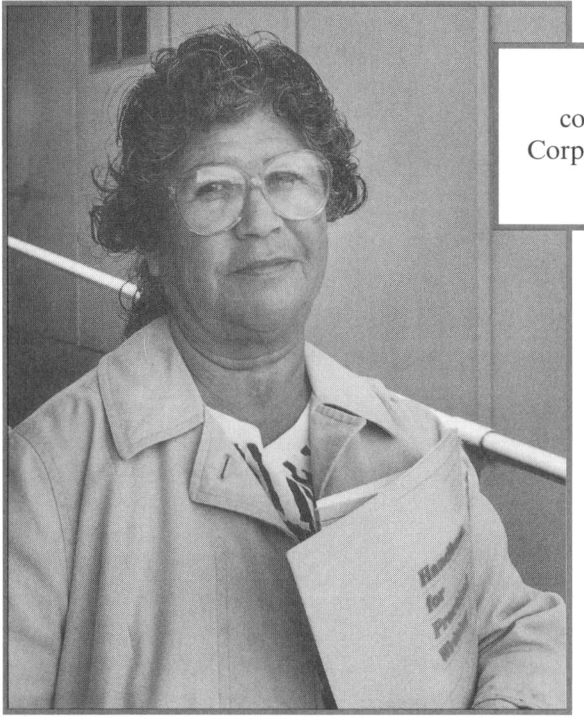

Maria Munoz studies English in a computer lab and a class through the Corpus Christi Literacy Council. Maria would like to get her GED.

I started to work when I was about nine years old. My dad died, so we had to learn how to work. There were 12 brothers and sisters in our family and all of us went to work. It was an adventure.

We went to work near Fort Worth. The first job we had was picking cotton. It was very hard for us because, at first, we didn't know how to do it. We picked about 50 pounds of cotton at a time and it was too much for us to carry. It was kind of hard for me because I was small, but my mom and my family tried very hard. The job didn't pay a lot. It was less than 25 cents a pound. We had to get up at 5 o'clock in the morning to get to work. We got to work at about 8 o'clock in the morning, and we worked until 3 o'clock.

IDIOM
kind of

Mexico and Texas have argued about, modified, and shared a border for hundreds of years. In this long association, people on both sides of the border have also shared language, food, and music. The very popular "Conjunto" music uses accordion, 12-string guitar, bass, percussion, and other instruments.

I went to school a little, but my family had to take me out. I didn't have any shoes to go to school. I had to go out in the fields barefooted. Sometimes it was cold, and I didn't even have a coat. We went from place to place to work in the Rio Grande Valley. We worked in the cabbage, carrot, and potato fields. In the Valley we didn't have any school at all.

I wished I was able to go to school more, but at the same time, I was learning outside. I was learning things—like how much the boss was going to pay us. We had to work very hard, but it was for food to eat, so we had no choice.

I used to work in a tortilla factory in San Diego, Texas when I was eleven years old. I had to grind the corn, boil the corn, and make the tortillas. I also had to do all the cleaning. I earned a dollar from 5 o'clock in the morning until 8 o'clock at night. My boss, Mr. Marroquin, and his wife helped me, so we all worked together. They taught me how to run the business.

I was already married when my family and I went to Michigan. We worked in the cherries and strawberries in Coloma, near Grand Rapids. Each year we had to stay about two and a half months because we had to come back to Texas in September to register our kids for school. We had nine kids. They all worked except the baby who stayed back in Texas.

I am very proud. I learned how to work very young. I speak Spanish at home, but my daughters speak English, and my grandchildren speak English. I've been hard-working all my life, but it has been good because we had to learn through life how to live. Here I am, 62 years old—hard-working and earning only a little, but still alive.

In Maria's life, what ways have school and work been connected? How do you think Maria feels about her work life? Explain your idea.

PROVERB

English: Work and saving are the best lottery.
Spanish: El trabajo y la economía son la mejor lotería.

2 Playing with Story Language

A. Maria Munoz is a **hard-working** and **proud** person. Even though she is over 60 years old, Maria is also very **active.** Reread the story and find words and phrases that demonstrate these characteristics.

hard-working ____

____

proud ____

____

active ____

____

B. Work with a partner to write a list of questions you would like to ask, if you could meet Maria.

____

Reading Strategy
Good readers connect their own experiences with what they read.

____

____

____

____

C. After you've finished your list, explain to others what questions you wanted to ask. Did you have similar questions?

Indirect Questions
I wondered **if** Maria likes computers. I asked when the class starts.
In an indirect question, the noun clause begins with **if, whether (or not)**, or a **wh-question word**, the verb follows the noun, and a period ends the sentence.

D. Do you know an older person in your community? Ask some of the same questions you wanted to ask Maria. Share the answers with your class.

3 Doing It in English: Interviewing for Jobs

A. Imagine you are the personnel manager of a successful and expanding computer store. Prepare a list of questions, direct or indirect, to ask the prospective employee.

OR

Imagine you are the prospective employee. Prepare a list of questions about job requirements, responsibilities, wages and benefits, and opportunities for advancement.

B. With a partner, roleplay a job interview. Take turns performing both parts. After you've practiced enough to feel comfortable, have a classmate or the teacher videotape the interview so you can see and hear your own language.

4 Journal Writing

In your journal, choose one of the following topics to write about:

1. Maria Munoz is an example of a hard-working, proud, and active older person. Write about a person you know who shows these same characteristics. Use specific examples to describe this person.

2. Maria considers herself a successful person. In what ways are you (or have you been) a successful person? Be specific.

PROVERB
English: Where the attempt is, there the success is, too.
Thai: ความพยายามอยู่ที่ไหน ความสำเร็จอยู่ที่นั่น

Learning Strategy
Knowledge is available everywhere, not just in school. Notice where and from whom you are learning, and start writing down what you learn in a notebook.

Other Voices from North America

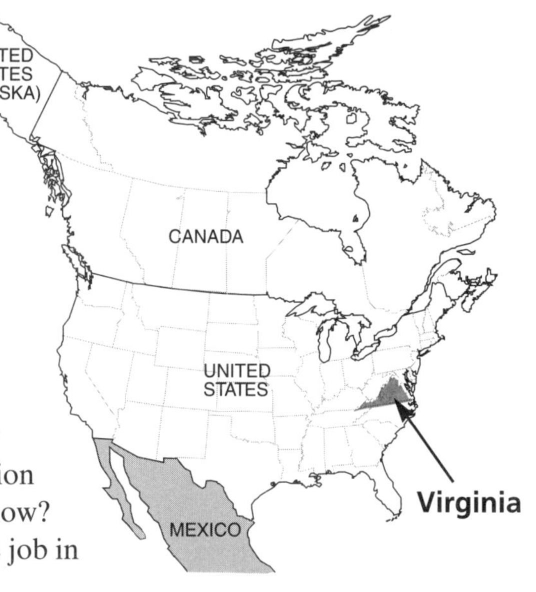

A. Look at the photographs of Cesar and Delilah. What do you think their jobs are? Explain.

B. When you read the following stories, compare your progress toward your own employment and education goals to Cesar's and Delilah's. Do you have a job now? How did you get it? Do you want to have the same job in five years?

Cesar Huamani lives in Fairfax County, Virginia.

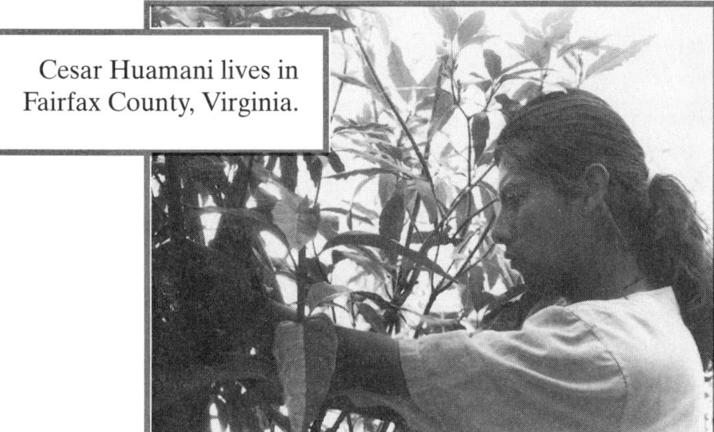

Reading Strategy

Learn the specialized vocabulary of your job or hobby. Learn what the words mean, how to spell them, and how to pronounce them. Use the dictionary, a book on the subject, or ask an expert.

After I graduated from high school, I went to work in the American Embassy in Lima, Peru. I was in the Commercial Department, Library Section. Being in the library section, I was forced to study English and the computer. Years later, because of a bad economic situation in my country and my parents' concern about my sisters' welfare, they decided to leave the country. Because my father worked for the American Embassy for more than 20 years, he got resident visas for the whole family.

My father went first with my older sisters. Then my little sister wanted to go. She was 15 years old and she wouldn't be able to go unless somebody older was by her side. That older person was I. My mother asked me to go with my sister. "I don't want to go," I cried. But she was persistent. When I finally decided to go, she had already packed my things in a small suitcase days earlier. At first I didn't want to go, but I believed that deep in my heart I did want to go. I didn't realize that until years later, living here.

IDIOMS
deep in my heart
kind of

I started to work for a small landscaping company; I kind of liked it. Then two years later, my friend, who owned the company, offered to transfer the ownership of the company to me, and he showed me how to do that. Now I am the owner of C&C Landscaping Service.

Peru is the third largest country in South America. Almost 45 percent of its people are Native Americans. Many of these people, who speak Quechua or Aymara, are descendants of the Incas, who were conquered by Francisco Pizarro in the 1530s. In 1821 Peru declared its independence from Spain.

We do landscaping for commercial and residential areas. My crew and I go to different places in the Washington Metropolitan Area. We see different kinds of gardens and each one has its own way to show its beauty. When I saw the other guys doing the work with the plants and dirt, I wanted to do the work with them and not just work as the boss. I have learned to love the plants. I know about the bushes: azaleas, photinias, hollies. We plant bulbs, and I am getting to know more about the perennials like columbines and astilbe.*

I love to work with Mother Nature and what I like most is her beauty. This is why I am going to NOVA (Northern Virginia Community College) to study computer to design landscaped areas and then horticulture to know more about it. Later, I would like to transfer to the University of Maryland to complete my education for my own self-esteem. I've seen a lot of designs in the gardens I've worked in, and I feel that I can do that work very well.

IDIOM
Mother Nature

* These are names of plants. Look in your dictionary to learn how to pronounce them in English.

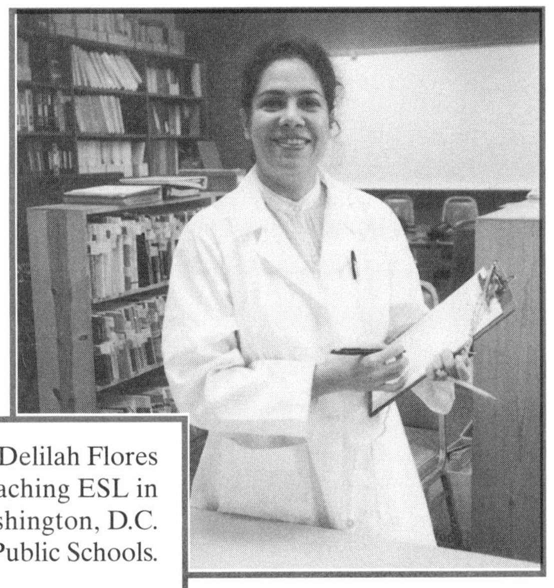

In 1995, Delilah Flores began teaching ESL in the Washington, D.C. Public Schools.

I completed my degree in Venezuela. I studied five years in the university to be a chemistry teacher. After that, I was working for three years at the high school level. I enjoyed working with teenagers, but after I worked with adults, at REEP (Arlington Education and Employment Program) I enjoyed that more.

My primary goal was to complete my Master's degree in biochemistry here.

I'm working as a clerk. I work with the microfilm. I develop the film, and then I retrieve the documents from the film I have already developed. I'm working for an insurance company. I've been there for about a year. It's very boring because you are doing the same thing all day long. Everything is production; you don't think, you just do it, that's it. It's not the way I have been brought up. I need to use my mind. That's why I am taking classes at night. I can't stop working, but I need to do something with my brain. I'm looking for a job as a medical technologist, working in a lab. I have done that job here, helping my sister as a volunteer and I have some experience that makes me feel confident enough to look for something in that field. I am also applying in Arlington Public Schools and Washington D.C. Public Schools to have the opportunity to teach.

Has having a good education from their native countries helped Cesar and Delilah here? In what ways?

Venezuela is a diverse country that includes a powerful petroleum industry, the urban capital of Caracas, and the Yanomami people of the Orinoco River Basin. The Orinoco River is the eighth longest river in the world. The Orinoco and the Amazon River form the largest river system in the world.

6 Doing It in English: Talking About Goals

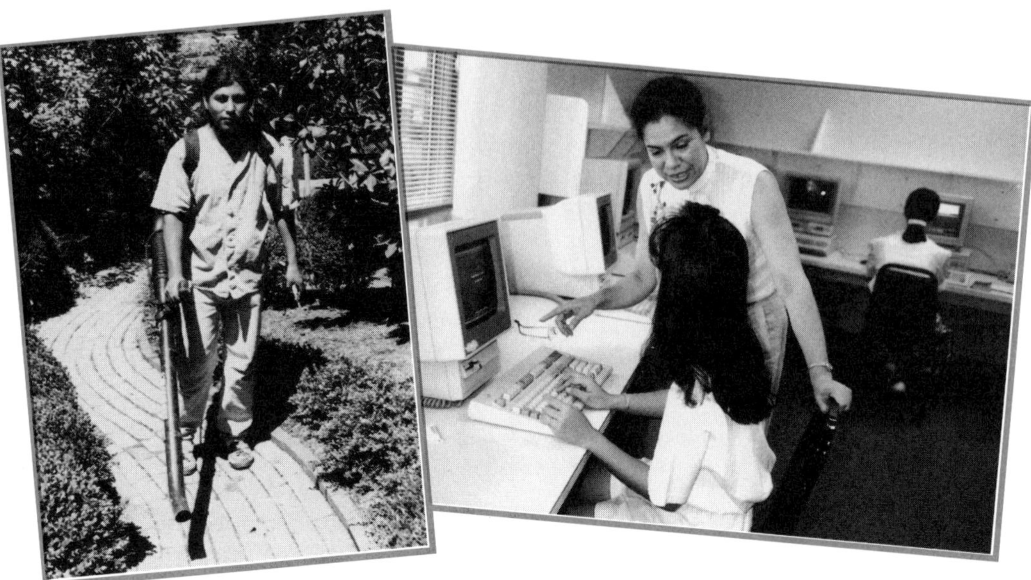

A. Both Cesar and Delilah have goals for themselves for school and work. They have short-term and long-term goals. Work with a partner to make a list of Cesar's and Delilah's goals. When you agree with each other, share your list with the class.

Learning Strategy
Dividing your goals into short-term and long-term goals helps you to remain realistic. Short-term goals are those you can accomplish in the near future. Long-term goals are your hopes and desires for your life.

B. Think about your own future. List your goals for work.

Short-term Goals	**Long-term Goals**
____________________	____________________
____________________	____________________
____________________	____________________
____________________	____________________

C. There are many ways to talk about goals:

I want to	I hope to
I'm going to	My plan is to
My idea is to	My goal is to
If I can, I will	My dream is to ____________________

D. Interview some of your classmates about their goals.

Name	What are your short-term goals?	What are your long-term goals?	What things can you do to reach your goals?

E. Looking at the answers to the chart questions, work with a small group to decide:

- Which goals seem most practical and realistic? Why do you think so?
- Do you think short-term goals should be more practical than long-term goals? Why or why not?

Together, write a paragraph that summarizes the group's conclusions. It's not necessary for each group member to agree. Read the paragraph to the rest of the class.

Learning Strategy
When you summarize an article or a conversation, you need to be objective. Personal opinions are not usually included in a summary.

PROVERB
English: To the stars through adversity. **Latin:** Ad astra per aspera.

7 Bringing the Outside In: Gathering and Sharing Information

A. With the whole class, brainstorm a list of work-related topics. These should include **interview techniques** and **advice on where to look for jobs.**

____

____

____

____

____

____

____

____

____

Learning Strategy

Being successful at work and finding new employment opportunities are partly the result of knowing where to look and what information to look for.

B. Choose one of the topics for a five to ten minute oral presentation. When you have chosen a specific topic, begin your research in the community.

Community Resources	
Library	Job Fairs
Job Counselors	Employment Service
Community Organizations	Internet
Experienced Workers	Newspapers

C. When you have some useful information to share, write an outline, and add details. Then, with a partner, practice giving your presentation. If you find any helpful flyers, cassettes, or videos, share them during your talk.

Learning Strategy

An outline can be written in many forms, but it needs to show the purpose, the introduction, the main points, and the conclusion of your presentation or paper.

D. Take turns giving the presentations. Ask and answer questions about the presentations.

Ideas for Action: Sharing for Power

A. With the class, make a file or lending library of the job-related materials you gathered for your oral presentations.

Word Formation
My **short-term** goal is to get a job. I'm going to a lecture on **job-related** skills.
Sometimes, new adjectives are formed by joining a noun + an adjective with a hyphen. If you are not sure of the form, consult your dictionary.

B. With the class and the teacher, make a "job opportunity" bulletin board. Divide the bulletin board into categories: **Job Information, Skills and Services Available** and **Help Wanted.** Put up the information the class has gathered, information about what skills you have, and job opportunities you know about. Maybe you can share the bulletin board with your whole school.

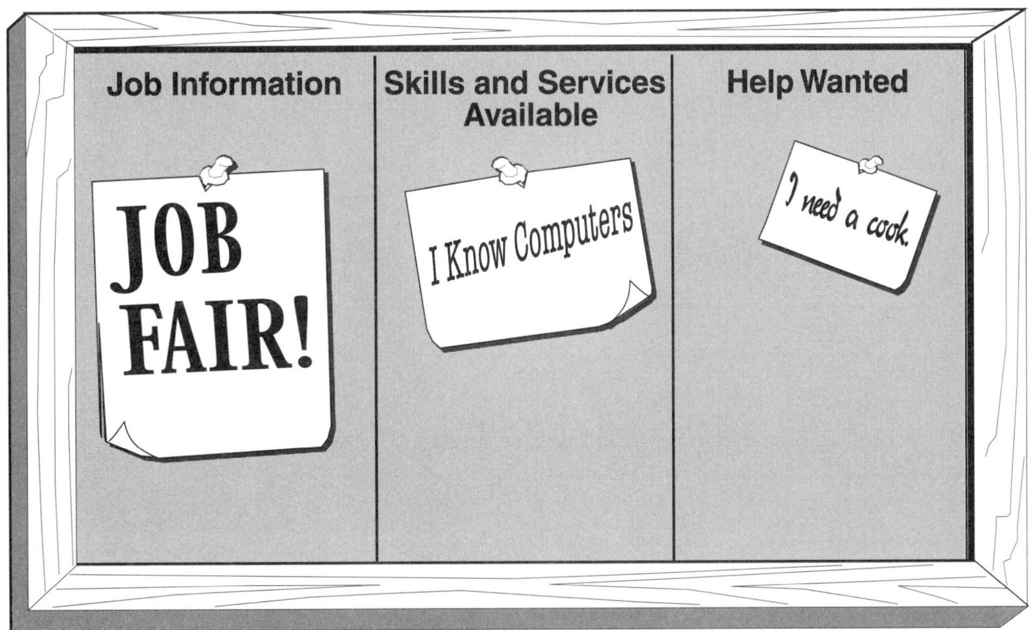

PROVERB
English: Knowledge is power. **Spanish:** Saber es poder.

9 Other Voices: The Poetry, Prose, and Music of Work

A. Because work is one of the basic elements of life, many varieties of writing reflect ideas and feelings about work. While you read the American examples below, compare the ideas and emotions expressed with those of your native language.

B. Although some words may be unfamiliar, see how much you can understand from context alone.

1

Early to bed, early to rise
makes a man
healthy, wealthy, and wise.
Benjamin Franklin

2

All work and no play
makes Jack a dull boy.
Nursery Rhyme

3

A MAN WORKS
FROM SUN TO SUN
BUT A WOMAN'S WORK
IS NEVER DONE
An old saying

4

His father works some days for fourteen hours
And you can bet he barely makes a dollar
His mother goes to scrub the floors for many
And you'd best believe she barely makes a penny
Living just enough, just enough for the city . . .
from the song:
"Living for the City"
Stevie Wonder

5

Now some people say a man's made out of mud,
But a poor man's made out of muscle and blood,
Muscle and blood, skin and bones,
A mind that's weak and a back that's strong.

CHORUS:
You load sixteen tons and what do you get
Another day older and deeper in debt,
Saint Peter, don't you call me 'cause I can't go,
I owe my soul to the company store.

from the song:
"Sixteen Tons"
by Merle Travis

6

The Ant and the Grasshopper—Once upon a time there were two insects who were friends: an ant and a grasshopper. It was summertime and the weather was warm, sunny, and pleasant. The ant worked hard. He carried food into his home all day long. The grasshopper said, "Why don't you quit working so hard and relax with me? It's a beautiful day and we can just eat when we are hungry." The ant refused. He said, "I must prepare for the winter when the weather will be cold and we can't go outside to gather food." So the ant worked, and the grasshopper played. When winter came, the ant was comfortable in his cozy nest and his stomach was full. The grasshopper knocked on his door and begged to come in. The ant was kind, so he let his friend share his home and food. But he scolded his friend. He said, "You are lazy and irresponsible. You should have worked and prepared for hard times. Now, you know better." **From Aesop's Fables**

IDIOM
know better

Reading Strategy

When you read a poem, a song, or a fable, look for the "moral" or lesson you are supposed to learn.

What lesson did you learn from this story?
Do you know this story or one like it?
Who told you the story?

10 Sharing Ideas: Mood, Rhythm, and Meaning

A. Choose one of the readings to study closely. Read the passage. Read it, again, out loud to yourself, a partner, or your teacher.

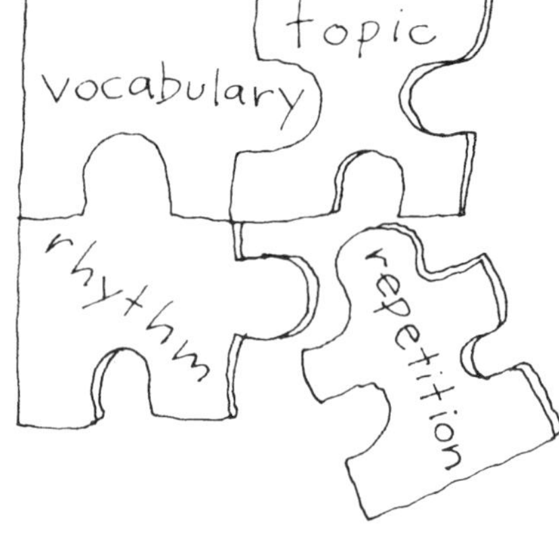

B. Now, answer the questions about the passage you studied. There might be more than one correct way to answer each question. Try to answer in complete sentences.

What is the **mood** of the passage?
Is it happy, sad, bitter, or philosophical?

____

____

Reading Strategy
You can understand the emotions, or **mood,** expressed in a piece of literature by analyzing such things as topic, vocabulary, rhythm, and repetition.

What words or word patterns give you clues to the meaning of the text?

____

____

Can you identify a pattern or rhythm in the words or sentence patterns? What elements make the pattern?

C. Talk to a student who read the same text as you did. Does he/she agree with your answers?

D. Choose your favorite text and paraphrase it. Read your words to the class.

____

____

____

____

____

____

Learning About Each Other: Cultural Sayings About Work

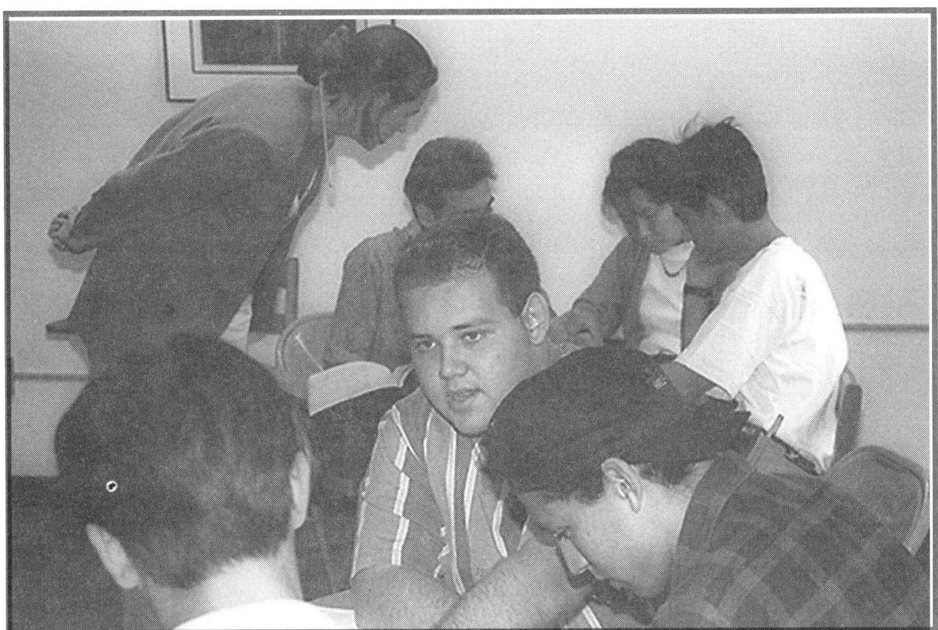

A. Do you and your classmates share some of the same feelings about work as each other and the texts? Think about some expressive idioms, poems, stories or songs from your native language that comment about work. Write it in your native language, then write it in English.

B. Ask a partner to help you to edit your English writing to make it clear and correct.

Learning Strategy
When you edit, don't forget to check the basics: spelling, capitalization, punctuation, pronoun reference, and subject-verb agreement.

C. With the whole class, decide how to produce the writing: in a book, on a bulletin board, or sharing a performance at your local community center.

12 Think It Over: Varieties of English

A. In Maria's, Cesar's, and Delilah's stories, each has a slightly different style. In the other readings, the style, vocabulary, and grammar are much different. Work in a small group to discuss opinions about English. Use some of the following statements to get you started:

Learning Strategy
Find friends who speak different varieties of English. Ask for help understanding pronunciation and idioms that differ from standard English.

Standard English is the only correct English.

American English is not as formal as British English.

You can't learn to speak English well if you practice with immigrants and other people with accents or dialects.

There is no reason to learn "street" English.

It's no good to read English literature that contains slang.

A person can't learn a language well without knowing all the grammar.

To get a great job, a person can't have a strong accent.

B. After talking with your group, ask your teacher to put up three signs around the classroom: **AGREE, DISAGREE,** and **UNSURE.** When a classmate or the teacher reads each statement, stand near the sign that expresses your opinion. Write the results on the board.

C. For the bulletin board, compile a list of what the majority of the class agrees about regarding the English language. Also, leave room on the bulletin board for alternative opinions that the class discussed.

IDIOM
leave room

Agreeing, Disagreeing, and Being Unsure		
Agree:	**Disagree:**	**Unsure:**
I agree with you (or with that idea).	I don't agree.	I can't decide.
I think that's true.	I'm not sure I can agree with that idea.	I'm just not sure.
I think that's right.	I can't agree with that completely.	I think I need some more time to think about this issue.
You've expressed my idea perfectly.	I'm afraid we are not in agreement.	

Options for Learning: Finding Employment Success

A. How do you want to be able to use English to help in employment? Check (✔) your answers. Add other ideas if you wish.

	Already Do	Want to Learn	Not Interested
Speak well and be confident in an interview.	______	______	______
Ask complex questions on the job or applying for a job.	______	______	______
Explain short-term and long-term goals.	______	______	______
Find employment information in your community.	______	______	______
Other? ______________	______	______	______

Looking Back

Think about your learning. Complete this form. Then tell the class your ideas.

A. The most useful thing I learned in this unit was ______________________________

____.

B. I would still like to learn ______________________________.

C. I learned the most by working

_______ alone. _______ with a partner. _______ with a group.

D. The activity I liked best was 1 2 3 4 5 6 7 8 9 10 11 12 13

because ______________________________.

E. The activity I liked least was 1 2 3 4 5 6 7 8 9 10 11 12 13

because ______________________________.

Learning Log

Checklist for Learning

I. Vocabulary: Add more words and phrases to each list. Check(✔) the ones you want to remember. For extra practice, write sentences with the new words and phrases.

Words to Describe People

_____ proud
_____ persistent
_____ __________
_____ __________
_____ __________
_____ __________

Employment

_____ résumé
_____ interview techniques
_____ __________
_____ __________
_____ __________
_____ __________

IDIOMS

_____ kind of
_____ __________
_____ __________

Occupations

_____ migrant worker
_____ medical technologist
_____ __________
_____ __________
_____ __________
_____ __________

PROVERBS

_____ To the stars through adversity
_____ __________
_____ __________
_____ __________
_____ __________

Words to Describe Language

_____ mood
_____ slang
_____ __________
_____ __________
_____ __________
_____ __________

II. Language: Check (✔) what you can do in English. Add more ideas if you wish.

I can

_____ write different kinds of questions to get information
_____ practice the kind of language used for job interviews
_____ roleplay to practice complex language situations
_____ use specific examples and language to describe a person I know
_____ ask and answer questions about short-term and long-term goals
_____ find employment information from a variety of sources
_____ give a five to ten minute oral presentation to the class
_____ __________
_____ __________

III. Listening: Listen to the Review Interview at the end of Unit 4. Ask your teacher for the *Collaborations* worksheet.

Special Communities

Refugees in Comer and Atlanta, Georgia

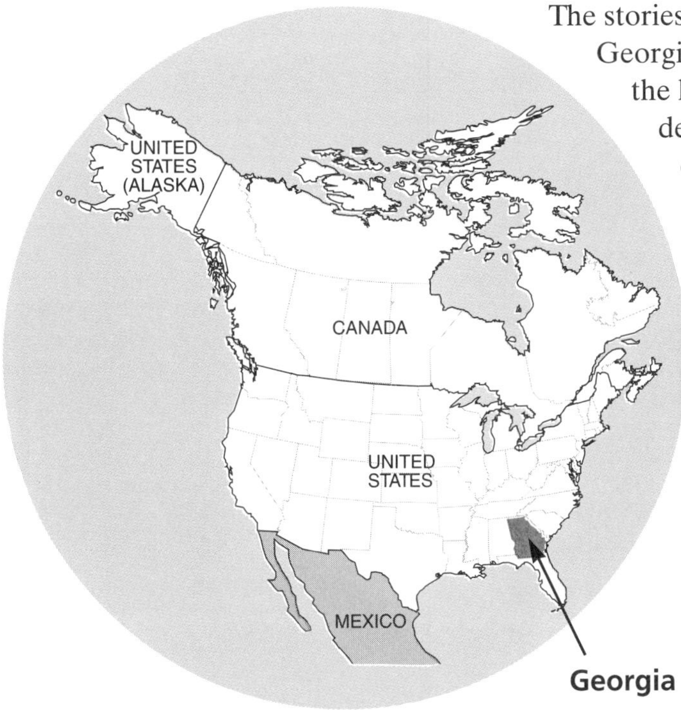

The stories in this unit are from Comer, Georgia and Atlanta, Georgia. Comer is a small town 75 miles east of Atlanta. It is the home of Jubilee Partners, a Christian community dedicated to helping others and living simply. Jubilee established a Refugee Welcome Center in 1979. Refugees stay for two to three months, study English, and learn about life in the United States. Since 1979, almost 2,000 refugees have come to Jubilee. During this time more than 300 volunteers from all over the world have worked there teaching, doing construction, gardening and maintenance work. Many of the refugees resettle in the Atlanta area.

UNITED STATES (ALASKA)
CANADA
UNITED STATES
MEXICO
Georgia

Stories from Jubilee: Enver Softic and Senita Roje

A. Discuss these questions with your class: What is a refugee? What is a volunteer? How much did you know about the United States before you came here? Did your expectations differ from reality?

B. Read the stories. Compare your early experiences in the United States to the writers' experiences.

Enver Softic, his wife Samka and daughter Elvedina are from Bosnia. They came to Jubilee before settling in Atlanta where Enver's brother is already living.

We have been here seventeen days. Jubilee people and my relatives, who are already living in Atlanta, met us at the airport. We didn't expect my relatives to be there. We arrived at Jubilee at 1 A.M. and we were surprised that people stayed up to meet us. At night we couldn't see anything but in the morning we woke up and looked around. It was so peaceful and natural.

We feel comfortable at Jubilee. The partners* and volunteers here are good people. They take us everywhere and they help prepare us for our life in Atlanta. We visit places, play soccer, and go fishing. We don't have the city crowd here and we don't worry about anything. We study English, but it is very hard for me and my wife because we are older. I know a little German, but I think I will learn English slowly.

We don't know much about Atlanta yet, but anything will be better than before. Before the war, our community in Bosnia was super. We could go everywhere and not be afraid of guns. We could sleep out in the yard. We could open our house to our friends.

Why does Enver feel comfortable at Jubilee?
Would you feel comfortable in a place like Jubilee?

*Partners are the people who are permanent members of the community. They live and work at Jubilee year round.

I have been in the United States for only one month and I came right to Jubilee. Many people have information about the United States in Bosnia through television, movies, newspapers and books. I thought I knew everything, but I didn't know what awaited. I did not expect to be living in a rural place like Jubilee. I expected to be living in an apartment in Atlanta right away.

Jubilee is different. My first day here I saw trees and animals and I felt the fresh air and the quiet. Sometimes I think time has stopped here. My people have a very strong pain. Sometimes it is difficult for us but the people here help us by being so nice. Also, here life is easy. Here I can take long walks and think. I have so many things to think about. I can talk with people and I can relax.

I study English here but I think I learn most of my English after class when we socialize and just talk to the volunteers.

Yesterday I visited Atlanta and saw many of my people. I think I am prepared to go now. I don't know about my future. What I want and what I must do are two different things. I must speak better English. I must work. I must stop dreaming. I *have* stopped dreaming. Slowly I stopped because reality is different from my dreams.

I would like to live like I did in Europe before the war. I needed only a few months more to finish college. I would like to teach Bosnian children or American children. Children are children. I would like this so much. I want to find a job in Atlanta that fits my personality. Something where I am with many people, like in a boutique.

Senita Roje is from Bosnia. She is living and studying English at Jubilee. She plans to settle in Atlanta.

How did Jubilee help Senita?
How is your arrival similar to or different from these stories?

Reading Strategy

To summarize, find the main idea and details that are necessary to understand the story. A summary is objective and does not include the reader's reactions.

C. Summarize the stories in your own words.

Playing with Story Language

Who, what, where, when, why, and **how** questions ask for information. They ask for details in a reading.

For example: **Where** is Enver from? Enver is from **Bosnia.**
Bosnia is a detail from the story.

A. Write five information questions for each story.

Enver Softic's Story

1. ______________________________

2. ______________________________

3. ______________________________

4. ______________________________

5. ______________________________

Senita Roje's Story

1. ______________________________

2. ______________________________

3. ______________________________

4. ______________________________

5. ______________________________

B. Ask a partner to answer your questions. Check your partner's answers.

Bosnia and Herzegovina was part of the former Republic of Yugoslavia. Since the spring of 1992, the country has been involved in civil strife among different ethnic groups. Many people have died and family members have been separated from each other. The international community has been trying to find a peaceful solution to the conflict.

3 Learning About Each Other: Our Lives Here

A. Work with a small group and find out about each other's first few months in the United States.

Name	Who helped you the most? How?	How did you learn about American culture?	How did you find out about English classes?

Senita Roje says that what she wants to do and what she must do are two different things.

B. List things that you *want* to do and things that you *must* do.

Want	Must
______________________	______________________
______________________	______________________
______________________	______________________
______________________	______________________

Expressing Obligation and Desire	
Obligation	**Desire**
I must cook dinner now. **I have to** cook dinner now.	**I want to** eat at a restaurant. **I would like to** eat at a restaurant.
Must and **have to** are used to express obligation. **Want to** and **would like to** express desire.	

Journal Writing

In your journal write about **one** of the following:

1. Has life in the United States been what you expected it to be?
2. Think about someone who helped you when you first arrived. Who was this person? How did he/she help you?

Doing It in English: Asking for Help

A. Read the conversations. Practice different ways to request help and respond to requests for help.

Requests with Would, Could, Can, and Will	
Would you please **Could** you please **Can** you **Will** you	open the door for me?
The verb that follows *would, could, can,* and *will* is in the simple form.	

IDIOMS
give a hand
hook up
don't mention it

Responding to Requests with *"Would you mind"*		
Request	**Can help**	**Can't help**
Would you mind driving me to school?	No, I wouldn't mind at all. No. I'd be happy to drive you.	Sorry, I can't because . . . I'd like to but I can't because . . .
To respond to a request for help using **would you mind,** answer "No" if you want to help. This means you don't mind or that it is not a problem for you.		

B. With a partner, create a conversation asking and responding to requests for help. Role play your conversation for your class.

6 Think It Over: Reading Graphs and Tables

Reading Strategy

Bar graphs can be used to show quantities. You must read two scales: the **horizontal → scale** and the **vertical ↑ scale.** These scales are labeled to tell you what the graph is measuring.

A. Graphs and tables give you information in a short, clear visual way. The following graph and table give information about immigration in the United States.

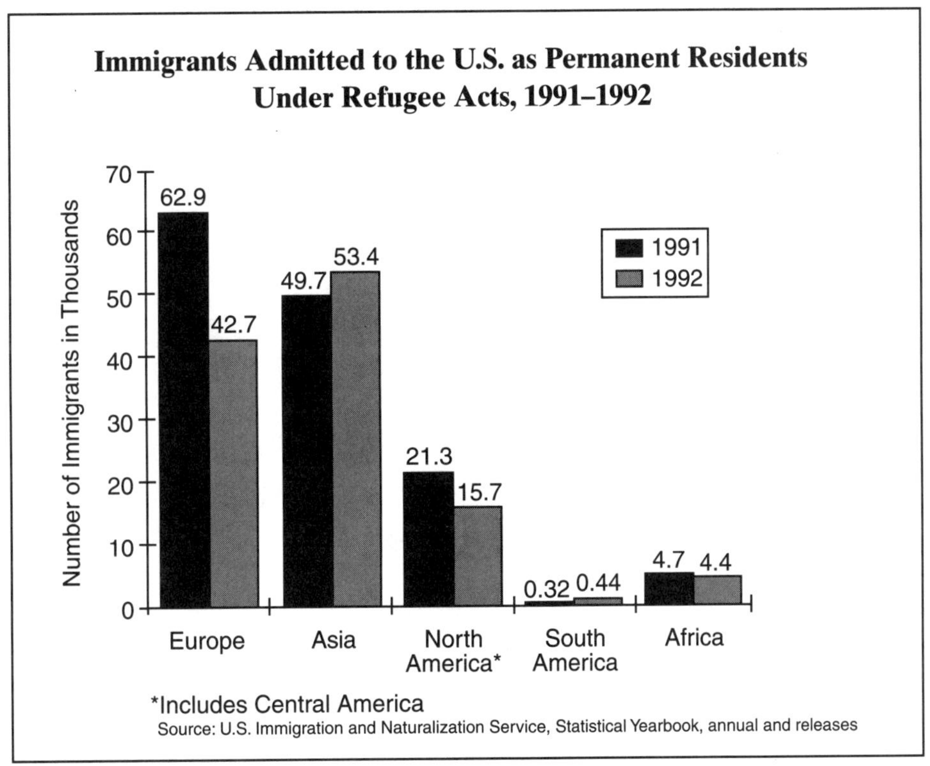

B. Read the bar graph to answer the questions. Check your answer with your partner.

1. What is the topic of the graph? ______________________
2. What does the vertical scale measure? ______________________
3. Was there an increase or a decrease in the number of refugees admitted to the United States in 1992? ______________________
4. Where did most of the refugees come from in 1991 and 1992? ______________________
5. Which continent had an increase of refugees admitted to the United States in 1992? ______________________

An opinion poll is a survey of what people think about a topic. A small part of the population answers questions and this information gives us an idea of what the general population may be thinking. Gallup is one company that gets information about public opinion. In 1993 the Gallup Poll survey asked the following question:

"How important—very important or not important—do you think each of the following factors should be in determining whether or not people from other countries should be admitted to live in the United States?"

The table shows the results of the poll.

Reading Strategy
Look at the **title** and the **headings** of each category to learn what kind of information is given in the table.

Factors for Admission to the United States—Gallup Poll 7/93 to 11/93

FACTORS	*Very important*	*Not important*	*No opinion*
They should have occupational skills.	78%	21%	1%
They should have relatives who are American citizens.	56%	42%	2%
They are facing religious persecution.	65%	32%	3%
They are suffering from economic hardship.	47%	49%	4%
They have money to invest in business in the United States.	50%	48%	2%
They are facing political persecution.	64%	31%	5%

C. Look at the table and discuss these questions in a small group.

1. What is the topic of this table?
2. What did the people interviewed think was the most important factor? Why do you think this was the most important one?
3. What did the people interviewed think was the least important factor? Why do you think this one was not as important?
4. Which factor do you think is most important?

7 Other Voices from North America: Being a Volunteer

A. Work in a group with other students. Read **one** of the following stories. Practice retelling the story in your own words with your partners. Be sure to retell the important points. *Remember, you are the experts for this story.* When everyone is ready, change groups. Form new groups of four people with one person from each of the original groups. Tell them about the story you read. Listen to them tell you about the stories they read.

Vlasta Zhang (third from the left) is from Croatia and has lived in the United States for four years. She has been a volunteer at Jubilee Partners for two years. She was a chemist in her country.

1. When I arrived in the United States, I came as a tourist. I came to visit friends. It was my choice to visit the United States, but the Bosnian refugees who came here had no choice. They *had* to change where they lived. I volunteer as a translator because the Croatian and Bosnian languages are very similar.

I always try to put myself in the refugees' position. I ask myself what I would need and want if I were in the same situation. Much of my work is just listening. When they are sad, I cry with them. When they are happy, I laugh with them. After they move to Atlanta, they call me up to tell me all about their new lives. They say, "Vlasta, guess what? I got a new car!" or "Vlasta, guess what? I got a new hair cut!" They call and tell me when their children do well in school. We remain friends.

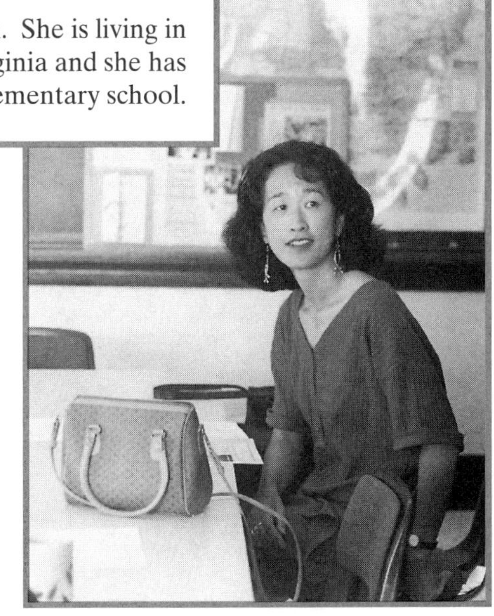

Chiyo Yasuda is from Japan. She is living in Charleston, West Virginia and she has volunteered at the local elementary school.

2. The first year I was in Charleston, I volunteered as an exchange teacher. I taught Kindergarten through sixth grade. I had fifteen classes and I taught each class for 45 minutes, once a week. I taught them about Japan and the Japanese language. I was so impressed because the children were so smart and so sweet. I was scared at first that maybe they wouldn't like a Japanese person but I never felt prejudice from them. None of them were mean to me. I had a good experience.

3. I volunteer with the American Red Cross. The first project I worked on was putting together school kits for Somali children living in refugee camps. Also, I'm vice-president of the Friends of Togo organization. This group was set up by Peace Corps volunteers who used to work in Togo. We give aid to Togo for small development projects. I volunteer to help people out. I've had an interest in working with international organizations for a long time. It's something I enjoy. People ask me how I find the time. I just say that if it's important for you to do something, then you will do it. It means being organized and scheduling things, but I just make sure I set aside the time for my volunteer work.

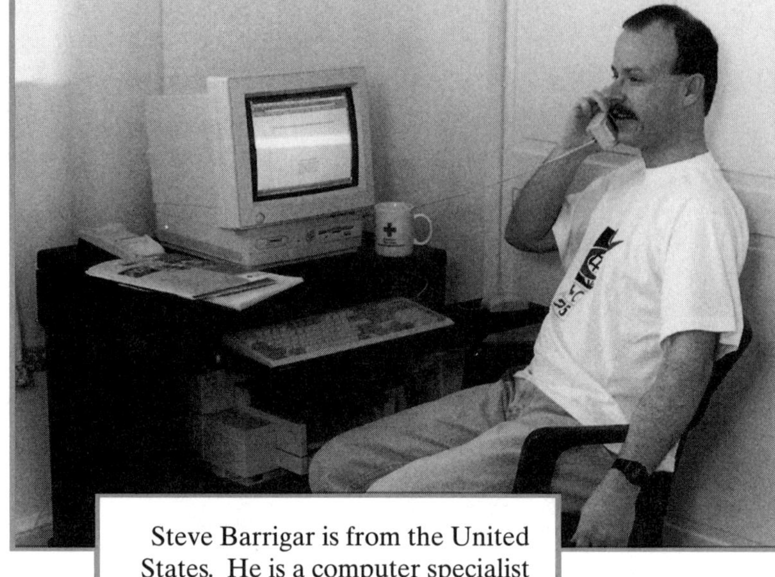

Steve Barrigar is from the United States. He is a computer specialist in Washington, D.C. He is studying for his Master's Degree in International Transactions.

Marcos Almanza came to the United States from Bolivia. He is a construction worker and lives in Arlington, Virginia.

4. I volunteer my time with *Desarrollo Comunal* which helps raise money for our village back home in Bolivia. We do this by having soccer tournaments with teams representing other Bolivian villages. With the money, we have been able to build a water tower, a plaza, and a small clinic. I also volunteer with the American Indian Society of Washington, D.C. I volunteer with them because I am interested in learning about the north side of American Indian culture. Our cultures are similar. Some of my people think it is bad to be an Indian, to speak Quechua or to be Incan. Those kinds of attitudes make me want to show them that it is not bad. I volunteer because I like it. I like to help people. That was the way I was raised. My mother was like that. She used to help a lot of people who came from the mountains. When I see something that I can do, I just say to myself, okay, I will do it.

B. List three facts you remember about each volunteer without looking at the stories. Compare your answers with those of members of your group.

Vlasta Zhang

____

____

____

____

Chiyo Yasuda

____

____

____

____

Steve Barrigar

____

____

____

____

Marcos Almanza

____

____

____

____

Japan is an island nation located east of Korea surrounded by the Sea of Japan and the Pacific Ocean. More than 125,000,000 people live there. It is called the "Land of the Rising Sun" and its flag shows a red sun on a white background. Japan has one of the most powerful economies in the world and is a leader in technology.

8 Ideas for Action: Getting Information

A. Several countries are mentioned in the stories of the volunteers. Can you locate the countries on a map?

B. What do you know about these countries? What would you like to know? Where can you get more information? Complete the table below.

Country	I already know	I want to know	Sources for information
Croatia			
Bosnia			
Japan			
Somalia			
Togo			
Bolivia			

C. Use your list of sources and get information about one country.

D. Report your information to the class.

Learning Strategy

When giving a written or oral report, choose a topic that interests you and keep it short and specific. Don't try to answer too many questions at one time.

9 Bringing the Outside In: Asking Questions

Choose **one** of the following with your class.

1. Take a poll with your class, decide on a topic, and write a question about the topic. Ask friends, co-workers and family members their opinions. Bring your results to class. Make a table graph showing the results.
2. Interview someone who does volunteer work. Before doing the interview, brainstorm with your class to get ideas for questions you could ask. Share your information with the class.

10 Doing It in English: Offering to Do Something

A. People offer to do something in many different ways. Brainstorm with the class. Can you think of expressions you have heard people use when offering, accepting, or declining help?

Let me help you with those packages.
Thank you.

List as many as you can.

____

____

____

____

____

B. Work with a partner to create conversations for the following situations. Show the class.

Example

A woman is talking to her friend on the telephone.

WOMAN: *I fell off a ladder and broke a bone in my foot. I have to wear the cast for six weeks.*

FRIEND: *Can I help you with anything?*

WOMAN: *Would you mind getting me a few things at the grocery store?*

FRIEND: *I'd be happy to. What do you need?*

WOMAN: *Just some milk, coffee, and bananas. Thanks so much!*

Thank you!

Spanish: *Gracias*
Croatian: *Hvala*
Mina (Togo): *Apke*

Somalia is the easternmost country on the African continent. The capital is Mogadishu. Most of Somalia lies on a plateau. It is cooler and has more rainfall there than on the coast along the Indian Ocean. In general, the climate is hot and dry. Recent civil conflict has caused many Somalies to flee their country to neighboring countries, Europe, and the United States.

Scene: Two strangers meet in a parking lot.

Scene: Two students are studying together.

The Republic of Croatia gained independence from Yugoslavia on June 25, 1991. It shares a border with Hungary, and the now independent states of Bosnia and Herzegovina, Serbia, Montenegro, and Slovenia. The Adriatic Sea borders Croatia in the east. The capital is Zagreb, an historic city with architecture dating back to the fifteenth century. Croatia is an important industrial and mining center, but the political instability in the region has caused economic and political problems.

Options for Learning: English in the Community

A. How do you want to get information about your local community services? How do you want to practice English in your community? Check (✔) your answers. Add others if you wish.

	Already Do	Want to Learn	Not Interested
Locate information about community services from the telephone book	________	________	________
Call for information about community services	________	________	________
Identify opportunities to volunteer in your community	________	________	________
Locate community places on a map	________	________	________
Other? ________________	________	________	________

B. Tell a partner or the class what you already do and what you want to learn.

C. Ask your teacher for a *Collaborations* worksheet to work on one of these goals.

12 Looking Back

Think about your learning. Complete this form. Then tell the class your ideas.

A. The most useful thing I learned in this unit was ____

____.

B. I would still like to learn ____.

C. I learned the most by working

________ alone. ________ with a partner. ________ with a group.

D. The activity I liked best was 1 2 3 4 5 6 7 8 9 10 11

because ____.

E. The activity I liked least was 1 2 3 4 5 6 7 8 9 10 11

because ____.

Learning Log

Checklist for Learning

I. Vocabulary: Check (✔) the words you know. Add more if you like.

Describing Places

_____ quiet
_____ natural
_____ ______________
_____ ______________
_____ ______________
_____ ______________
_____ ______________

Describing Feelings

_____ surprised
_____ comfortable
_____ ______________
_____ ______________
_____ ______________
_____ ______________
_____ ______________

IDIOMS

_____ give a hand
_____ hook up
_____ ______________
_____ ______________
_____ ______________
_____ ______________

II. Language: Check (✔) what you can do in English. Add more ideas if you wish.

I can

_____ express obligations.
_____ express desires.
_____ ask for help.
_____ offer to do something for someone.
_____ accept and decline an offer of help.
_____ summarize a reading passage.
_____ retell a story in your own words.
_____ read bar graphs and tables.
_____ write questions about a reading passage.
_____ ______________________________
_____ ______________________________

III. Listening: Listen to the Review Interview at the end of Unit 4. Ask your teacher for the *Collaborations* worksheet.

Staying in Touch

Stories from Laos and California

Laos is a small country located in Southeast Asia between Thailand and Vietnam with a population of approximately 4,440,000. The capital of Laos is Vientiane, which is located on the banks of the Mekong River. More than half of the population of Laos is made up of ethnic minorities living in the remote mountainous regions of the country. These groups include the Hmong, Mien, Yao, and Khmu.

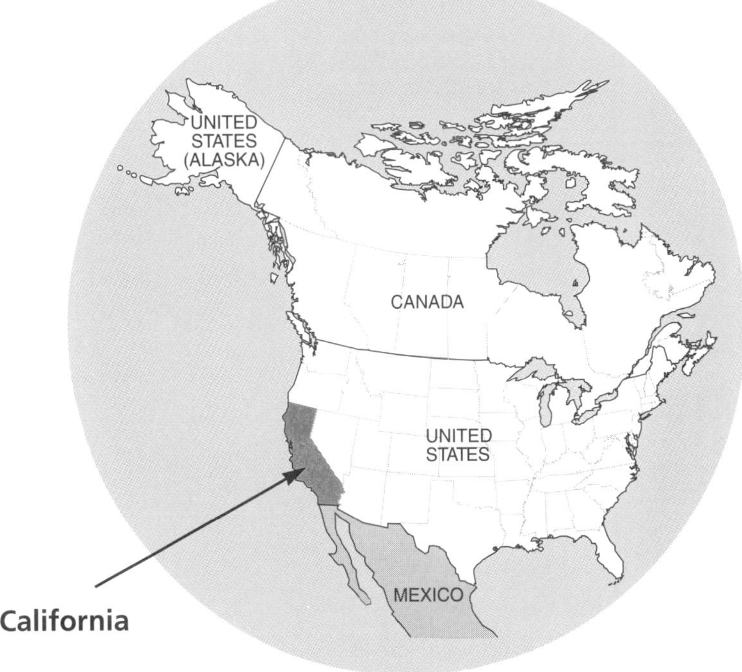

California

Los Angeles is located on the coast of southern California, on the Pacific Ocean. With a population of approximately 3,485,000, Los Angeles is the second largest city in the United States. The people of Los Angeles are ethnically diverse, with rapidly growing Korean, Mexican, and Southeast Asian immigrant communities. Los Angeles is the center of the entertainment industry and the home of many famous movie and television stars.

The Dengvilay Family Story

A. Look at the photos on this page and the next page. How are the people in the photos alike? How are they different? Discuss the similarities and differences with your classmates before you read the stories.

PART 1: Luang Prabang, Lao People's Democratic Republic

All of our children are grown now. Five of them live in America, and five still live in Laos. One of our daughters spent six years studying in Russia. The two youngest are not married yet, so they still live with us in Luang Prabang. Our oldest daughter is married to a Japanese man who owns a Sushi restaurant in Los Angeles, California. The seventh one lives in Los Angeles, too, with her husband and two young children. We feel very happy whenever we hear from them. They write letters and send us pictures of our new grandchildren.

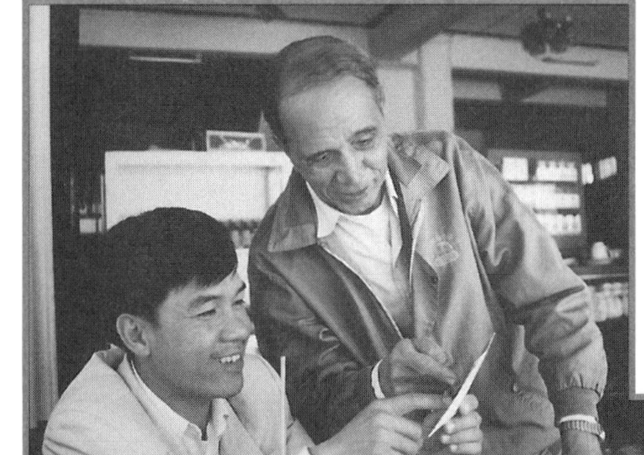

Mr. Dengvilay owns a furniture shop in Luang Prabang, Laos. Keo Phovilaichit lives in Sydney, Australia. In this photo, he is translating a letter from Mr. Dengvilay's granddaughter.

We Lao people love our families very much. Not a day goes by that I don't think about our children, even if they are halfway around the world. Of course, they write us letters in Lao, but our grandchildren can write only in English.

This letter arrived about six months ago from our granddaughter in Texas, but we weren't able to read it for a long time. We can speak French quite well, but not a word of English.

A few days ago, our neighbor's son came home for a visit. He lives in Australia now. He said he would be happy to translate the letter for us.

In Laos, we take care of our parents when they get very old. My mother still lives with us. Everyone here calls her Grandmother Pheng. She is 95 years old, but she is still in good health. She was married to a Frenchman, but he died when I was a young boy. She never told me much about my father, but I know she remembers him. She helped raise most of our children because my wife and I were so busy in those days.

After 1975, life became very hard for us here in Laos. That's why five of our children decided to leave. We worried about them night and day. We were really upset when we heard that our oldest daughter got robbed! Last year was a lucky year for us because two of our daughters came back to Laos to visit us. We hadn't seen them for more than ten years. How grown up and successful they looked! We hope that the others will be able to come home someday, too.

Mr. Dengvilay's youngest son, Saisana, with Grandmother Pheng.

PART 2: Los Angeles, California

Four of Mr. Dengvilay's grown children gather at Bouakham's home in Los Angeles. From left: Bouaket, Bouachan, Bounthavy, and Bouakham

Bouachan's Story

In Laos, I was a teacher. I used to be fluent in French, but I've forgotten most of it now. Here in America, I'm a business person. I run a Sushi restaurant in Los Angeles with my husband. He's Japanese. Life is pretty good here most of the time, but I miss my parents and friends in Laos. I wish we could all be together. I'm very close to my sisters and brothers, and I'm glad that we live in the same area so we can visit each other often.

The worst thing that happened to me was when I got robbed a few years ago. I had just come back from work and opened the door to my bedroom. Then this guy jumped out. He told me to lie down on the floor and he put a towel over me.

I told him, "Go ahead, take anything you want, but don't hurt me."

He told me not to move until he said it was OK. Then I waited. I was too scared to do anything. I kept waiting, but still he didn't say anything. Nothing happened. Finally, I asked him, "Hey! Are you OK?"

There was no answer, so I turned my head and looked up. He was gone, and so was everything else except my wedding ring! Still, it was a close call. I'm happy that I didn't get hurt. I was lucky. It could have been much worse. It's better to lose everything as long as you keep your life.

In Laos, most people think it's easy to get rich in America. They don't know how hard it is. I may go back to live in Laos someday, but probably not until I get a lot older. Then maybe I'll want to go back for good. If I went back now, I'd have to start all over again.

Next year, we are planning to bring our parents to California for a visit, just for a couple of months. I don't think my mom would want to stay here forever, though. She enjoys spending a lot of time at the temple with her friends. That's the way most of the older ladies in Luang Prabang spend their time, getting ready to pass on to the next life. It wouldn't be easy for her to do that here.

IDIOMS
for good
pass on
close call

- What do you remember best about your country?
- How do you stay in touch with your family and friends back home?
- Do you ever plan to return? When?
- Have you ever had a close call? What happened? What did you learn from it?

Sharing Ideas: Story Reactions

A. The Dengvilay Family Story was told by two people: Mr. Dengvilay in Laos, and his eldest daughter, Bouachan, in Los Angeles. Use the information below to help you remember each part. Then take turns retelling the parts of story from each person's point of view.

Reading Strategy
Recognizing a writer's point of view helps you understand the story better.

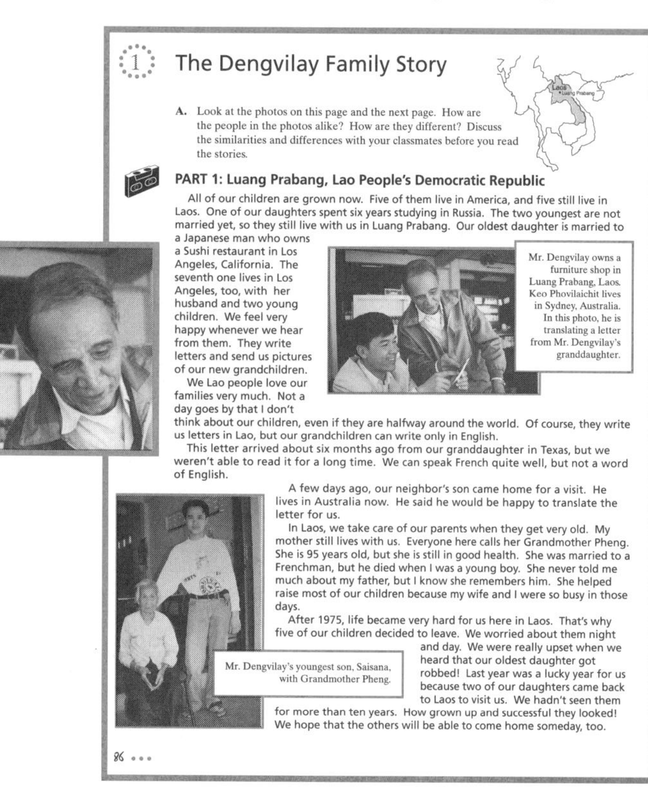

1 The Dengvilay Family Story

A. Look at the photos on this page and the next page. How are the people in the photos alike? How are they different? Discuss the similarities and differences with your classmates before you read the stories.

PART 1: Luang Prabang, Lao People's Democratic Republic

All of our children are grown now. Five of them live in America, and five still live in Laos. One of our daughters spent six years studying in Russia. The two youngest are not married yet, so they still live with us in Luang Prabang. Our oldest daughter is married to a Japanese man who owns a Sushi restaurant in Los Angeles, California. The seventh one lives in Los Angeles, too, with her husband and two young children. We feel very happy whenever we hear from them. They write letters and send us pictures of our new grandchildren.

We Lao people love our families very much. Not a day goes by that I don't think about our children, even if they are halfway around the world. Of course, they write us letters in Lao, but our grandchildren can write only in English.

This letter arrived about six months ago from our granddaughter in Texas, but we weren't able to read it for a long time. We can speak French quite well, but not a word of English.

A few days ago, our neighbor's son came home for a visit. He lives in Australia now. He said he would be happy to translate the letter for us.

In Laos, we take care of our parents when they get very old. My mother still lives with us. Everyone here calls her Grandmother Pheng. She is 95 years old, but she is still in good health. She was married to a Frenchman, but he died when I was a young boy. She never told me much about my father, but I know she remembers him. She helped raise most of our children because my wife and I were so busy in those days.

After 1975, life became very hard for us here in Laos. That's why five of our children decided to leave. We worried about them night and day. We were really upset when we heard that our oldest daughter got robbed! Last year was a lucky year for us because two of our daughters came back to Laos to visit us. We hadn't seen them for more than ten years. How grown up and successful they looked! We hope that the others will be able to come home someday, too.

Mr. Dengvilay owns a furniture shop in Luang Prabang, Laos. Keo Phovilaichit lives in Sydney, Australia. In this photo, he is translating a letter from Mr. Dengvilay's granddaughter.

Mr. Dengvilay's youngest son, Saisana, with Grandmother Pheng.

86 • • •

PART 2: Los Angeles, California

Four of Mr. Dengvilay's grown children gather at Bouakham's home in Los Angeles. From left: Bouaket, Bouachan, Bounthavy, and Bouakham

Bouachan's Story

In Laos, I was a teacher. I used to be fluent in French, but I've forgotten most of it now. Here in America, I'm a business person. I run a Sushi restaurant in Los Angeles with my husband. He's Japanese. Life is pretty good here most of the time, but I miss my parents and friends in Laos. I wish we could all be together. I'm very close to my sisters and brothers, and I'm glad that we live in the same area so we can visit each other often.

The worst thing that happened to me was when I got robbed a few years ago. I had just come back from work and opened the door to my bedroom. Then this guy jumped out. He told me to lie down on the floor and he put a towel over me.

I told him, "Go ahead, take anything you want, but don't hurt me."

He told me not to move until he said it was OK. Then I waited. I was too scared to do anything. I kept waiting, but still he didn't say anything. Nothing happened. Finally, I asked him, "Hey! Are you OK?"

There was no answer, so I turned my head and looked up. He was gone, and so was everything else except my wedding ring! Still, it was a close call. I'm happy that I didn't get hurt. I was lucky. It could have been much worse. It's better to lose everything as long as you keep your life.

In Laos, most people think it's easy to get rich in America. They don't know how hard it is. I may go back to live in Laos someday, but probably not until I get a lot older. Then maybe I'll want to go back for good. If I went back now, I'd have to start all over again.

Next year, we are planning to bring our parents to California for a visit, just for a couple of months. I don't think my mom would want to stay here forever, though. She enjoys spending a lot of time at the temple with her friends. That's the way most of the older ladies in Luang Prabang spend their time, getting ready to pass on to the next life. It wouldn't be easy for her to do that here.

IDIOMS
for good
pass on
close call

- What do you remember best about your country?
- How do you stay in touch with your family and friends back home?
- Do you ever plan to return? When?
- Have you ever had a close call? What happened? What did you learn from it?

• • • 87

B. Which part of the story was most interesting? Why? Retell the part you chose to a partner.

C. Do you have anything in common with the Dengvilay family? Check the sentences from the story that are also true for you. Discuss your responses with the whole class.

	True for me	Not true for me
Not a day goes by when I don't think about our children.	❑	❑
We take care of our parents when they get very old.	❑	❑
Last year was a lucky year.	❑	❑
Life is pretty good here most of the time.	❑	❑
Maybe when I get a lot older, I'll want to go back for good.	❑	❑
It's better to lose everything as long as you keep your life.	❑	❑

Playing with Story Language

A. A storyboard is a sequence of pictures and words used to plan movies and television dramas. Listen again as Bouachan tells the story of the robbery. Think about how this story might be made into a storyboard.

B. Rewrite the scene of the robbery in the form of a storyboard. Imagine that your storyboard will be used to produce an action packed movie or television show. Write the words you think Bouachan and the robber said or thought on the lines below each picture.

What's going on here?

C. Share your storyboard dialogues with another set of partners. How is this scene similar to scenes you have seen in a movie or on TV? What did Bouachan learn from her experience? Why is it often helpful for victims of crimes such as these to share their stories with others?

Sharing Experiences: Imagining What We Would Have Done

A. Think about Bouachan's experience and how she felt after it was over.

"I'm happy that I didn't get hurt. I was lucky. It could have been much worse. It's better to lose everything as long as you keep your life."

Bouachan Dengvilay with her sister and niece at the Thai Buddhist temple in Los Angeles.

B. Get together with a small group of your classmates. Discuss what you would have done in her place.

Using Conditional Sentences to Talk About Past Possibilities
She **could have tried** to get his gun away. I **would have given** him all my money.
Past conditional sentences describe past situations in which the facts are changed. In these types of sentences, the main subject is followed by a modal (*would, could, might*) + have + the past participle form of the verb.

C. Tell the group about a close call or another interesting thing that happened to you. Explain what you learned from the experience. Invite the members of your group to tell what they would have done in your shoes.

IDIOM
in (someone else's) shoes

D. In the space below, summarize one of your classmate's stories. Tell briefly what happened, what he or she learned, and what you would have done.

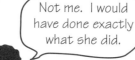

Example: Suhair got lost in downtown Los Angeles late at night. She asked a policeman for help. I would have done exactly the same thing.

____

____

5 Learning About Each Other: Prospects for the Future

A. Do you remember what Bouachan said about going back to live in Laos?

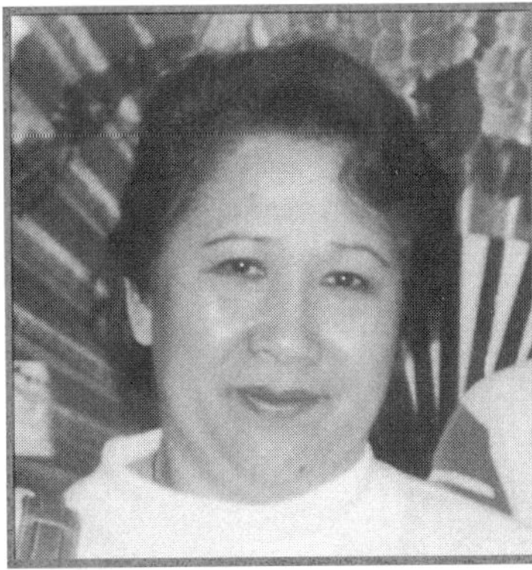

"If I went back now, I'd have to start all over again."

B. Tell the group something you probably *won't* do in the near future, and explain why. Make a list of your group's statements, including your own.

I probably won't move very far from Los Angeles because I want to stay near my family.

____

____

____

____

C. Ask other group members to explain their statements using sentences like this.

If I moved away, I wouldn't be able to visit my family very often.

Using Conditional Sentences to Discuss Future Possibilities
If she **went** back to Laos now, she **would have to** start all over again. If I **bought** a new car, I **couldn't pay** all my other bills.
Conditional sentences are sometimes used to talk about future possibilities. In these sentences, *If* is followed by the past form of a verb, even though it refers to present or future action. The second part of the sentences use *would, could,* or *should* to introduce the imagined result.

Elena probably won't move very far away from Los Angeles because if she did, she wouldn't be able to visit her family and friends.

D. Ask one classmate to read your group's statements and explanations to the whole class.

6 Doing It in English: Expressing Wishes

A. If you had three wishes, what would they be? Read Bouakham's answer.

First, I wish I could go back home to visit my grandmother again. And I wish my children could come with me so they could see where we are from. My third wish is one for the whole world—I wish there would never be another war.

Bouakham Dengvilay is Bouachan's younger sister. She immigrated to the United States in 1981. Today, she lives in Los Angeles with her husband and two small children.

B. Tell a partner about three wishes *you* have. Make a "wish list" for you and your partner.

Expressing Wishes
I wish I **knew** the answer. We wish we all **could be** together again. He wishes he **were** rich and famous.
To express a wish in the present or future time, use the past plural form of a verb, even if the subject is singular. You can also use a modal such as *could* or *would* + a basic verb form.

Our Wish List
1. We wish we had more time to study.
2. We wish we had more money.

7 Journal Writing

Some people wish for things that cannot possibly come true, while others make more realistic wishes. What do you wish for most often? Why do you wish for it? What are the chances of it coming true? Let your imagination fly. Write about one or more of your favorite wishes.

Think It Over: Learning from History

A. The article describes a recent event and summarizes the history of modern Laos. Before you read, scan the article for the following information.

Year of Lao independence from France: ______________________

Name of the country after 1975: ______________________

Number of refugees who left Laos: ______________________

Reading Strategy

When you *scan* an article for specific facts, look only for the information you want to find. Then read the article to get the whole picture.

A Bridge to Peace

In its glory, Laos was known as "The Kingdom of a Million Elephants and of the White Parasol." In modern Laos, elephants have become a rare sight, and busloads of foreign tourists line up outside the gates of the former royal palace. After nearly twenty years of isolation from much of the world, with its economy at a virtual standstill, the country's leaders have taken the first cautious steps toward the twenty-first century. With the completion of the *Mithapap* (Friendship) Bridge in 1994, which connects Laos with a former enemy, the King of Thailand and the President of the Lao PDR (People's Democratic Republic) joined hands to symbolize the beginning of a new era.

Given the recent history of this tiny Southeast Asian nation, its leaders have every reason to be cautious. The country has periodically fallen under the domination of its more powerful neighbors, and was a French colony from 1893 to 1953. In 1944, a group of Lao patriots formed the *Lao Issara* (Free Laos) resistance movement. Supported by the international Communist movement, this group later became known as the *Pathet Lao.* Following the French departure from Southeast Asia in 1954, the *Pathet Lao* opposed the Lao Royal Government and the United States involvement in Southeast Asia.

The Mithapap (Friendship) Bridge was completed in 1994.

Although Laos struggled to remain neutral throughout the 1960s, the fighting between the Pathet Lao and the U.S.-backed Royal Government finally erupted into a full-scale civil war. The United States never officially entered the war in Laos, but instead carried on a "secret war," unknown to the American public. As part of this effort, U.S. military personnel provided equipment and training for Hmong fighters from the mountainous regions of the country to oppose the *Pathet Lao*. During this period American planes dropped more than two million tons of bombs over areas of the country that were under Communist control, causing immense destruction and loss of life.

When the United States pulled out of Vietnam in 1975, the King of Laos was forced to abdicate,[1] and the Lao PDR took control of the country, virtually shutting its doors to the West. Fearing reprisals, more than 400,000 refugees fled across the Mekong to camps in Thailand, and eventually to new homes in Western countries.

Laos has received substantial economic aid from Vietnam and the Eastern European countries, yet its per capita income[2] remained one of the lowest in the world. In 1989, when socialism began to collapse in Europe, the Lao leadership had begun to seek more aid and investment from the West. The *Mithapap* Bridge, jointly funded by Thailand, Australia, and Sweden, was built to help stimulate economic growth and promote friendly relations between Laos and Thailand, as well as with the rest of the world. In the meantime, the Lao government has also opened its doors to tourists and to former refugees wishing to return home. Since 1990, thousands of overseas Lao, who are now citizens of other countries, have returned to visit their families. Many have even invested in businesses and contributed to private development projects in their hometowns and villages.

[1] abdicate—to give up ruling power
[2] per capita income—(Latin) average income for each person

Keo Phovilaichit, standing on the right in this photo, works in an automobile factory in Sydney, Australia. He has returned to his hometown of Luang Prabang, the former royal capital of Laos, to visit his mother. When he saves enough money, Keo would like to start a business in Laos. Mr. Vilavong, on the left, is a weaver who sells baskets to tourists in Luang Prabang.

B. Reread the article carefully. Then discuss it with a small group of your classmates, using the questions below as a guide.

Learning Strategy

Discussing your reactions to a reading and identifying related issues can help you express your ideas more clearly.

- Why do you think the present leaders of Laos are cautious about establishing new relations with other countries?
- Name the two most interesting things you learned from this article.
- What other world events (past or present) are you concerned about? Make a list for further discussion.

C. The timeline below shows how events in Laos led up to war and the departure of more than 400,000 refugees. As you read over the timeline, use the map to help you locate key places.

1944	Formation of *Lao Issara* (Free Laos)
1953	Kingdom of Laos receives official independence from France
1954	French departure from Southeast Asia
1954–1957	*Pathet Lao* (Communist movement) gains influence in Laos
1957	Neutralist government established in Vientiane
1961	Agreements break down, U.S. "secret war" in Laos begins
1961–1975	Full scale civil war, backed by the United States and North Vietnam
1975	United States withdraws from Vietnam
1975	Lao People's Democratic Republic established
1975–83	400,000 refugees leave Laos for Thai border camps
1994	*Mithapap* (Friendship) Bridge completed

Learning Strategy

A **timeline** is a list of events in *chronological* order (the order in which they happened). A timeline based on a reading about history can help you understand the whole picture and recall important details.

The three-headed elephant, symbol of the former Kingdom of Laos, and the flag of the Lao PDR at the entrance to the National Museum.

D. Without looking back at the article, practice explaining the events in the timeline to a partner. Use the map and the photo on this page as you discuss events on the timeline. Then discuss these questions.

- What period of history does the timeline cover?
- What was going on in other parts of the world during the same period? List as many events as you can.

E. The tapestry in this photograph uses images, rather than words, to tell a story. Use the images in the tapestry to retell the story to a partner. Write your version of the story and read it aloud to another set of partners. Compare your different versions.

Hmong child in Luang Prabang, Laos (1971)

This tapestry was made by Hmong refugee women living in Minnesota. The Hmong are a minority people from the mountainous regions of northern Laos who speak their own language and have their own customs. Since 1975, approximately 100,000 Hmong have settled in communities across North America.

Learning About Each Other: Major Events

A. Think about an important event in your life. Write notes about the event on the left side of the experience chart.

B. Work with a partner. Ask about an important event in your partner's life. Take notes on the right side of the chart. Ask more questions about parts you don't understand or when you want further information.

Notes on an Important Event in My Life	Notes on an Important Event in My Partner's Life
Time and place	
What happened?	
How did you feel about it then?	
How do you feel about it now?	
Additional information	

Another Voice from North America

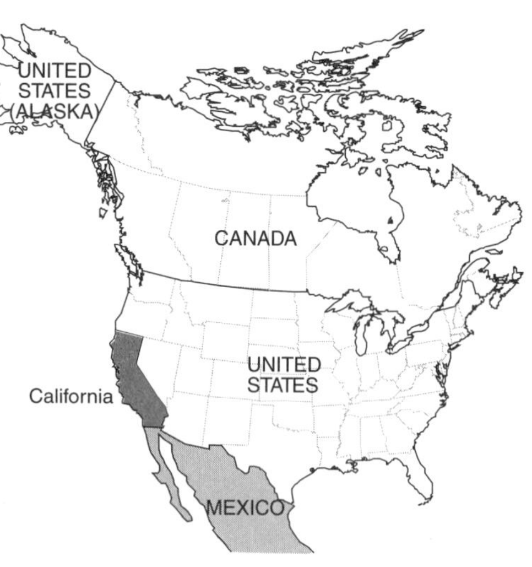

A. Read and enjoy Tsekyi Dolma's story. How does she stay in touch with the past?

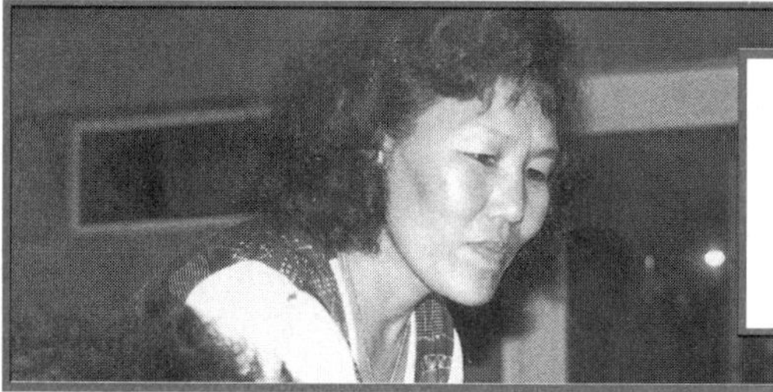

Tsekyi Dolma is a registered nurse. She lives in Fullerton, California with her husband and two children.

For over 30 years, I held pictures of Tibet in my memory, as clearly as if it were yesterday. I remember very dim mornings and crossing rivers with shimmering pebbles at the bottom. I went out with my brothers and sisters to tend the sheep and the yaks. We used to catch birds and put a little colored cloth on the wing or neck, then let it go. That way, we could see it flying and say, "this is the bird I caught, and I freed it. This is a sign that no one can kill this bird."

I don't have any memory of when I left Tibet, but I guess I must have been six or seven years old. Our family got separated, and I left Tibet with my mother and my two younger sisters. When we got to Nepal, we found out that the parents had to go to the labor camps, to build roads in India, and the kids were going to be sent to school. We all stood in line, and the parents had to go to one side, and the kids to the other. That is how my sisters and I got separated from our mother, and we never saw her again. She was not used to that kind of life, and they told us that she got lost. That's the only news we heard.

IDIOMS
in seventh heaven
package tour
bit by bit
no way

My sisters and I were sent to missionary school in India, and we stayed there for 16 years. We spoke Tibetan among ourselves, but we studied in Hindi. It was only after I got married and came to live in America that I started to improve bit by bit in the Tibetan language. I learned to read and write while I was pregnant with my first child.

In 1994, I decided to travel to Tibet. By that time, I had an American passport so I joined a package tour. It was the first time I had been back in more than 30 years. As soon as we landed in Lhasa, I couldn't believe it. Oh! The air was so fresh! I felt like I was in seventh heaven. I ran to the river and drank with my hands, and I never got sick.

About 85–90 percent of the population of Lhasa is now Chinese. It was hard to buy incense or white scarves to offer at the holy places because the shops are all Chinese.

The best part of the whole trip was seeing my relatives, the ones I hadn't seen for over 30 years. They were thrilled. They thought that we were dead, and had been performing special rituals for us each Tibetan New Year. But when I asked them if they would like someday to leave this place and go with us, they said, "no way!"

As for me, I'd love to go back and help Tibetans improve their lives, especially in medical care and education. When Tibet is free, I am sure we will all go back. Right now there are around 100,000 Tibetans in exile, and now we have become educated. We want to go back and build our country.

If you go to Tibet, it might change the way you see the world. I hope to go again, and I encourage all my friends to go, whatever the purpose. The experience will be so tremendous, just like falling in love.

B. What did you learn about Tibet by reading Tsegyi Dolma's story? Write three new pieces of information:

____

____

____

C. Use the information in Tsegyi Dolma's story to complete her personal time line.

D. Think about the major events in your own life. For each event, write down the date and a short note on what happened. Then make your own personal timeline to share with the class.

1959	______________________
1960	sent to missionary ______________
______	graduated from school
1978	qualified as a registered nurse
1980	married Nawang Phuntsog
1982	son, Tenzin, born
1983	immigrated to ______________
1986	daughter, Thupten, born
1990	received US citizenship
1994	______________________
1995	moved to California

Tibet is situated on a vast plateau, surrounded by the world's highest mountains. Although Tibet had existed since ancient times as an independent state, it was invaded by Chinese military forces in 1951 and claimed as part of China. A Tibetan rebellion against Chinese rule in 1959 resulted in the flight of the Dalai Lama, the Tibetan spiritual leader, and thousands of his followers to refugee communities in northern India, Great Britain, and the United States. The current population of Tibet is approximately 2,283,000.

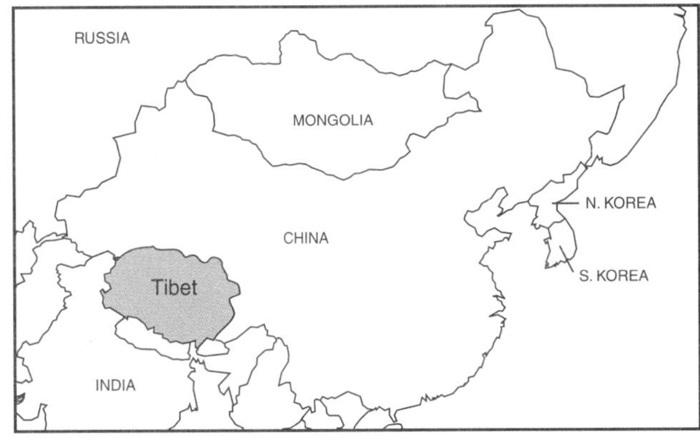

Proverbs About Home and Relatives

	Home is where the heart is. (USA)
ຕັດສາຍເລືອດບໍ່ໄດ້ເໝືອນດັ່ງຕັດສາຍນໍ້າ	Water can be diverted in many directions, but blood flows in a single stream. (Laos)
"Il n'est pire ennemie que ses proches."	There is no worse enemy than a close relative. (France)
རྡོ་ཆུང་ཆུང་རླུང་ལྷག་པས་འཁྱེར་དོགས་མེད་	Worry not! Strong winds cannot blow away small pebbles. (Tibet)

Bringing the Outside In: News from Home

Bring in a letter from a relative, a videotape, or a recent photograph from relatives or friends in your country. Share it with your classmates. Use maps, posters, or other visual aids that will help your classmates get the picture.

As you listen, take notes on any new information you learned from your classmates' presentations.

I learned that . . .

Lhasa is a city in Tibet.
____

____

____

Ideas for Action: Visit a Travel Agency

A. Plan to telephone or visit a travel agency.

Prepare questions about one or more of the following topics in advance.

1. the cost of a round-trip ticket to a country you would like to visit
2. documents needed for travel to this country (passport, visa, other papers)
3. legal restrictions or other problems for tourists or visitors
4. other helpful information

B. Share what you learned with the class.

Options for Learning: Staying in Touch

A. What do you want to be able to do in English?
Check (✔) your answers. Add other ideas if you wish.

	Already Do	Want to Learn	Not Interested
Plan a travel itinerary	______	______	______
Write a family history	______	______	______
Tell a group of Americans about your migration experience	______	______	______
Read current news articles about events in your home country	______	______	______
Other? ______________	______	______	______

Looking Back

Think about your learning. Complete this form. Then tell the class your ideas.

A. The most useful thing I learned in this unit was ______________________________

____.

B. I would still like to learn ______________________________________.

C. I learned the most by working

______ alone. ______ with a partner. ______ with a group.

D. The activity I liked best was 1 2 3 4 5 6 7 8 9 10 11 12 13

because ______________________________________.

E. The activity I liked least was 1 2 3 4 5 6 7 8 9 10 11 12 13

because ______________________________________.

Learning Log

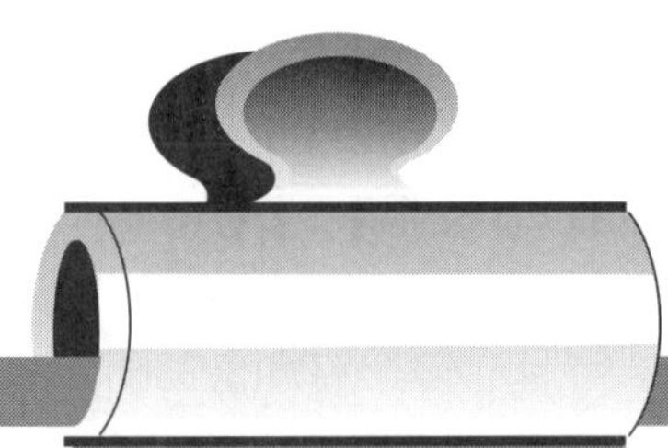

Checklist for Learning

I. Vocabulary: Add more words and phrases to each list. Check(✔) the ones you want to remember. For extra practice, write sentences with the new words and phrases.

Family Members

_____ children
_____ parents
_____ _______________
_____ _______________
_____ _______________
_____ _______________
_____ _______________
_____ _______________

IDIOMS

_____ a close call
_____ _______________
_____ _______________
_____ _______________

Continents/World Regions

_____ Southeast Asia
_____ Europe
_____ _______________
_____ _______________
_____ _______________
_____ _______________
_____ _______________
_____ _______________

Life Events

_____ birth
_____ wedding
_____ _______________
_____ _______________
_____ _______________
_____ _______________
_____ _______________

Phrases to Describe Historical Events

_____ a new era
_____ fall under domination
_____ _______________
_____ _______________
_____ _______________
_____ _______________
_____ _______________

II. Language: Check (✔) what you can do in English. Add more ideas if you wish.

I can

_____ relate an important event in my life
_____ share my reactions to a story
_____ explain what I would have done in someone else's place
_____ summarize someone else's story
_____ discuss wishes and prospects for the future
_____ scan an article for specific information
_____ use a time line to take notes on historical events
_____ _______________________________
_____ _______________________________

III. Listening: Listen to the Review Interview at the end of Unit 6. Ask your teacher for the *Collaborations* worksheet.

GLOSSARY OF GRAMMATICAL TERMS

adjective—word that describes a noun or a pronoun: a *beautiful* person, a *peaceful* country, it was *difficult.*

adverb—word that tells us more about a verb, an adjective, or another adverb: I *sometimes* write in English, a *happily* married couple, she sings *extremely* well.

article—word used to mark a noun. In English, there are three articles: *a*, *an* and *the*.

base form—simplest form of a verb: *see*, *ask*, *work*. Also called **simple form.**

clause—group of words containing a subject and a verb, and forming part of a sentence: *Before I came to the United States*, I studied English for just two months.

complement—word or words used after a form of *be* to complete the meaning of the subject. A subject complement is usually an adjective, a noun, or a noun phrase: I've been *hard-working* all my life. I was *an electrical engineer.*

conditional sentence—sentence that states a possibility, usually containing an if clause: *If you go to Tibet,* it might change the way you see the world. *If she went back to Laos now,* she would have to start all over again. *If she had tried to call the police*, the thief might have hurt her.

direct quote—the use of somebody's exact words. In writing, a direct quote is indicated by quotation marks ("   "): *"I don't want to go!"* he cried. Also called **direct speech.**

gerund—verb used as a noun; formed by adding *-ing* to the base form of the verb: She doesn't like *working* as a clerk. *Deciding* what to do is difficult sometimes.

indirect question—report of what somebody asked, not using their exact words. Indirect questions do not use questions marks: She wanted to know *when the game would start.*

infinitive—verb form that can function in a sentence as a noun. In English, infinitives are preceded by *to* and do not take endings (-s, -ing, or -ed): He would like *to become* a teacher.

modal—verb used with another (main) verb to add to its meaning. Modals include *can, could, may, must, ought to, will,* and *would.* Also called **modal auxiliary** or **helping verb.**

noun—word used to name a person, place, thing, or idea. My *parents* are originally from northern *India. Sincerity* is really important.

noun phrase—group of words acting together as a noun. He calls himself *a lucky guy.*

object—noun, noun phrase, or noun clause that receives the action of a verb: I had to grind the *corn*, boil the *corn*, and make the *tortillas*. I don't know *what you mean*. An object may also be part of a prepositional phrase: I expected to be living in an *apartment* right away.

passive—verb form that indicates that the subject of the sentence receives the action; passive forms can occur in any tense: The parade *is attended* by thousands of spectators every year; The poem *was written* by Mariano Ramos.

past continuous—verb tense expressing an action that began and ended in the past. Often used in sentences with the simple past to indicate that something was going on at the time another action occurred. She *was taking a bath* when the telephone rang. Also called **past progressive.**

past participle—verb form used mainly in perfect and passive verb phrases. Usually shows past or completed action: has *been*, had *gone*, was *taught.*

past perfect—verb tense expressing an action or situation completed before another action in the past: Maria *had worked* in the factory for several years before she learned to run the business.

past perfect continuous—verb tense expressing an action that continued over a period of time before another action began: They *had been living* in Michigan before they went back to Texas. Also called **past perfect progressive.**

phrasal verb—verb consisting of two words (verb + particle). Phrasal verbs have meanings that are different from the words that make them up, and many are considered idioms: *call up* (telephone), *give in* (surrender), *catch on* (understand).

plural—noun form indicating more than one of a kind; usually formed by adding *-s* or *-es* to the noun: *kids, carrots, peaches*. Some nouns, however, have irregular plurals: *women, people, children*; and some do not take plural forms: *cotton, money, air*.

preposition—word that shows the relationship between a noun and another part of a sentence. Common prepositions include *in, on, around, about, with, for,* and *to*.

preposition cluster—combination of an adjective and a preposition following a form of the verb be: She's *proud of* her children.

prepositional phrase—group of words containing a preposition, a noun, and any additional words used to describe or mark the noun. I'm taking classes *at night*. I need to do something *with my brain*.

present continuous—verb tense that expresses an action that is going on at the present time. Delilah *is working* in her office today. Also called **present progressive.**

present participle—verb form ending in *-ing*; usually used with *be* to show continuous action: They are *living* in Los Angeles now.

present perfect—verb tense that expresses an action or situation that has a strong connection to the present. Often used with *since* and *for*: She *has studied* English for three years (she is still studying it).

pronoun—word that takes the place of a noun, such as *she, him, themselves, my, it.* Most pronouns have different forms, depending on their use in a sentence.

pronoun reference—relationship between a pronoun and the noun it is taking the place of. To indicate this relationship clearly, pronouns are usually close to their nouns. We had nine *kids*. *They* all worked except the baby.

relative pronoun—words like *that, which,* and *who* that show the relationship of a descriptive clause to a noun in the sentence. I want my poetry to be understood by people *who* have no education at all.

relative clause—the whole clause, beginning with a relative pronoun, that describes the noun it follows. I want to find a job in Atlanta *that fits my personality*.

reported speech—retelling of what somebody said, not using their exact words: She told me *that she had worked in the strawberry fields.* Also called **indirect speech** or **indirect quote.**

simple future—verb tense that expresses expected action or condition in the future. Formed by combining *will* or *am/is/are* + *going to* + base form of the verb.

simple form—basic form of a verb: *see*, *ask*, *work.* Also called **base form.**

simple past—verb tense that expresses a single, completed action or situation that happened or was true in the past. Formed by adding *-ed* to a regular verb, or using the irregular past form. Yesterday I *visited* Atlanta and saw many of my people. I *saw* the trees and animals and I *felt* the fresh air and quiet.

simple present—verb tense that expresses an action or situation that is habitual (happens again and again) is true at the present time, or is always true. She *speaks* three languages. Children *are* children.

singular—noun form indicating one of a kind; *bridge, elephant, day*

subject—noun, pronoun, noun phrase, or noun clause that is the doer of the action expressed by the main verb. In English, the subject almost always comes near the beginning of a sentence: *Life* is pretty good here most of the time. *Not a day* goes by when I don't think about our children. *What I want* and *what I must do* are two different things.

subject-verb agreement—necessity for verbs to agree with their subjects within a sentence. In general, a singular or uncountable noun takes a singular verb: *The bride* usually *wears* a white dress; *Education is* the main goal. A plural noun takes a plural verb: My *parents are* originally from northern India.

uncountable noun—noun that represents a whole group or type of item, such as sugar, water, fruit. These nouns do not take plural forms. Also called **noncount** or **mass** nouns.

verb—word that expresses action or existence. My family *moved* here; They *are* students.

wh-question—question beginning with *what, when, where, whose, how,* or *why*. Also called **information question.**

COMMON IRREGULAR VERBS

Base (Present) Form	Past Form	Past Participle
awake	awoke	awoken
be	was, were	been
become	became	become
begin	began	begun
bite	bit	bitten (or bit)
bleed	bled	bled
blow	blew	blown
break	broke	broken
bring	brought	brought
build	built	built
buy	bought	bought
catch	caught	caught
choose	chose	chosen
come	came	come
cost	cost	cost
cut	cut	cut
dig	dug	dug
do	did	done
draw	drew	drawn
drink	drank	drunk
drive	drove	driven
eat	ate	eaten
fall	fell	fallen
feed	fed	fed
feel	felt	felt
fight	fought	fought
find	found	found
fly	flew	flown
forget	forgot	forgotten
forgive	forgave	forgiven
freeze	froze	frozen
get	got	gotten
give	gave	given
go	went	gone
grow	grew	grown
have	had	had
hear	heard	heard
hide	hid	hidden
hit	hit	hit
hold	held	held
hurt	hurt	hurt
keep	kept	kept
know	knew	known
lay	laid	laid
lead	led	led
leave	left	left
lend	lent	lent

Base (Present) Form	Past Form	Past Participle
let	let	let
lie	lay	lain
light	lit	lit
lose	lost	lost
make	made	made
mean	meant	meant
meet	met	met
pay	paid	paid
prove	proved	proven (or proved)
put	put	put
quit	quit	quit
read	read	read
ride	rode	ridden
ring	rang	rung
rise	rose	risen
run	ran	run
say	said	said
see	saw	seen
seek	sought	sought
sell	sold	sold
send	sent	sent
shake	shook	shaken
shine	shone	shone
shoot	shot	shot
shut	shut	shut
sing	sang	sung
sit	sat	sat
sleep	slept	slept
speak	spoke	spoken
spend	spent	spent
stand	stood	stood
steal	stole	stolen
swear	swore	sworn
sweep	swept	swept
swim	swam	swum
take	took	taken
teach	taught	taught
tell	told	told
think	thought	thought
throw	threw	thrown
understand	understood	understood
wake	woke	woken
wear	wore	worn
weep	wept	wept
win	won	won
write	wrote	written

INDEX

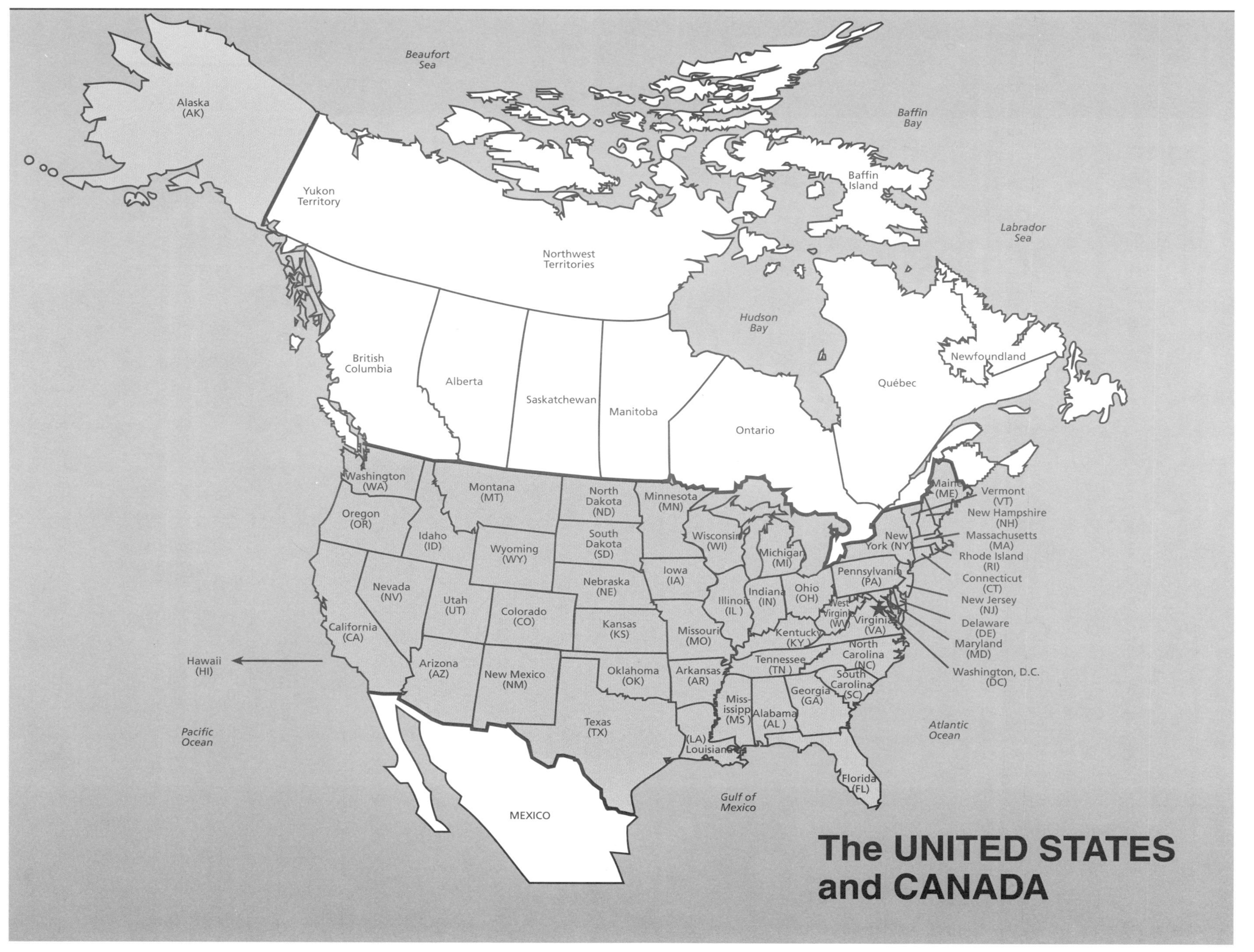
Beaufort Sea
Alaska (AK)
Yukon Territory
Northwest Territories
Baffin Bay
Baffin Island
Labrador Sea
Hudson Bay
British Columbia
Alberta
Saskatchewan
Manitoba
Ontario
Québec
Newfoundland
Washington (WA)
Montana (MT)
North Dakota (ND)
Minnesota (MN)
Oregon (OR)
Idaho (ID)
Wyoming (WY)
South Dakota (SD)
Wisconsin (WI)
Michigan (MI)
New York (NY)
Maine (ME)
Vermont (VT)
New Hampshire (NH)
Massachusetts (MA)
Rhode Island (RI)
Connecticut (CT)
New Jersey (NJ)
Delaware (DE)
Maryland (MD)
Washington, D.C. (DC)
Nevada (NV)
Utah (UT)
Colorado (CO)
Nebraska (NE)
Iowa (IA)
Illinois (IL)
Indiana (IN)
Ohio (OH)
Pennsylvania (PA)
West Virginia (WV)
Virginia (VA)
California (CA)
Kansas (KS)
Missouri (MO)
Kentucky (KY)
North Carolina (NC)
Hawaii (HI)
Arizona (AZ)
New Mexico (NM)
Oklahoma (OK)
Arkansas (AR)
Tennessee (TN)
South Carolina (SC)
Georgia (GA)
Mississippi (MS)
Alabama (AL)
Texas (TX)
Louisiana (LA)
Pacific Ocean
Atlantic Ocean
Florida (FL)
Gulf of Mexico
MEXICO
The UNITED STATES and CANADA